People are talking...

Make It Happen with Feng Shui™ is a plum of a resource for those looking to enhance their life and well-being. The combination of Feng Shui, emotional clearing, aromatherapy and crystals is powerful and effective."

—Katherine Ball
PSYCH-K® Facilitator and Feng Shui Consultant

"I love this book. *Make It Happen with Feng Shui*™ is so informative, complete and inspiring. There is so much valuable information people can apply that will make a difference in their lives. I highly recommend getting a copy for yourself, friends and family."

—Amanda Collins
Feng Shui Consultant

"Fantastic! What a wonderful jewel. *Make It Happen with Feng Shui*™ is user friendly, a great read and well-designed as a reference tool. Professional practitioners and those simply interested in bettering their lives will find great knowledge and useful tools. I love having the recipe for success and the ingredients so readily available!"

—Dana K. Race
Feng Shui Consultant and Motelier

"As a teacher and a 'facilitator of change' who has studied just about everything under the sun regarding transformation, I found Jen Leong's book to be well informed and dynamic. It is rare to find multiple transformational concepts and techniques together in one concise book. It pulls it all together in an easily read, neat little package. Change starts from within and as human beings, we each have a role to play in its transformation and healing. Jen has achieved just that with this book."

—Jennifer Buergermeister, M.A., C.Ht., D.D.
Spiritual Counselor, Feng Shui and Holistic Health Consultant

...make it happen!

attract what **YOU** want!

make it
HAPPEN
with feng shui

JEN LEONG, MA, HHP, NC

COSMIC CHI
PUBLISHING

Published and distributed in the United States by:
Cosmic Chi Publishing
11956 Bernardo Plaza Drive #107
San Diego, CA 92128

For more information, visit:
www.JenLeong.com

Edited by: Anita Edmondson
Interior Design by: Anita Edmondson and Susan Engbring
Illustrations by: Anita Edmondson
Cover Design by: Joy Chu
Author Photo by: Monique Feil

For more information on Feng Shui and Holistic Health, or other topics covered in this book, see the list of additional resources and websites located in the back of this book.

Library of Congress Control Number: 2010907018
ISBN 978-0-9796256-3-3

Leong, Jen.
    Make it happen with feng shui: attract what you want / Jen Leong.
ISBN 978-0-9796256-3-3

Contents

PART I: MASTERING THE FUNDAMENTALS

PART II: PUTTING THE NATURAL METHODS TO WORK

FOR FURTHER INFORMATION

My Journey

My journey started in Malaysia, where I was born and raised in an orphanage for almost eight years. I was fortunate to be adopted by an American family, who brought me to the United States and provided me with opportunities I would not have had otherwise. As an orphan in Malaysia, my fate would have left me out in the streets at the age of 13 to become a street sweeper. If I was lucky, I would have been picked up to sew in a factory. Although I encountered many challenges during my childhood, both at the orphanage and with my adopted family, I am grateful for those experiences which gave me the opportunity for personal growth and healing.

As a child, I was always interested in nature and drawn to natural ways of healing on all levels which has led me down a wide-ranging holistic career path. As a result, I have developed my own unique and powerful system that applies natural holistic methods to attract what you want.

I went to U.C. Davis where I graduated with a B.A. in Wildlife Biology. While I loved nature, certain methods of research did not resonate well with me. I decided to use my degree to teach Biology in the public schools and received my Teaching Credential a few years later. I then decided to pursue another passion of mine at the time, exercise and physiology. I received my Masters in Exercise Physiology and began a career in fitness training and nutrition. Soon clients were encouraging me to become a massage therapist too, so I could give them a massage after their workout! Sounded interesting, so I decided to pursue that avenue as well. Much to my amazement, I found a whole new world of holistic health when I took my first massage class. I discovered so many other healing modalities. It was like heaven to me. I could not get enough. I had to go further down that path!

After more than 1,000 hours of training, I became a Holistic Health Practitioner. I continued learning other holistic methods including Touch for Health, kinesiology (muscle testing), hypnotherapy, nutritional therapy, aromatherapy, crystal therapy and emotional clearing. I studied with prominent health figures including Dr. John Thie, Dr. James Durlacher, Dr. Brian Garrett, Dr. Bob Marshall, Dr. Dan Harper, Dr. Dale Schusterman, Dr. Dee Hahn, and Dr. Valerie Morton.

During my Holistic Health practice, I started hearing about environmental healing through something called Feng Shui. Another form of healing? I was intrigued. I knew I could use Feng Shui with my clients as another holistic healing tool on the environmental level.

I started my Feng Shui training with Terah Kathryn Collins at the Western School of Feng Shui™ and with Dr. Richard Tan, Feng Shui expert and Acupuncturist. Later, I studied Compass Feng Shui, including Eight Mansions and Flying Stars with Master Peter Leung with the School of Chinese Metaphysics and Yasha Jampolsky with the Green Planet School of Feng Shui.

To further enhance my Feng Shui training, I studied Space Clearing with Denise Linn and Feng Shui Real Estate with Holly Ziegler. Most recently, I have studied Fashion Feng Shui with Evana Maggiore, which combines Feng Shui principles with wardrobe planning to express our authentic self and our intentions.

In the process of conducting research and writing this book, I developed a line of Feng Shui aromatherapy called *Jewel Essence*®, which includes nine unique blends of essentials oils, one for each area of the Bagua Map and a special Space Clearing one. In Chapter 14, I reference some of these blends in a collection of success stories.

As a Feng Shui Consultant, Holistic Health Professional (HHP), Nutritional Consultant (NC), Speaker and Educator, I feel the experience, training and expertise I have gained over the past 18 years have helped me empower people with tools and techniques needed to bring health, harmony and transformation into all aspects of life. Friends, clients and colleagues agreed and suggested that I write a book. This book is another way for me to share my knowledge and help people enhance their lives through simple natural holistic methods with powerful results.

Looking back from when I was an orphan to where I am today—living a happy, successful life with a wonderful family—makes me a believer that you can make it happen and attract what you want.

Now, I invite you to start your own journey
towards enhancing your well-being and life goals.

Foreword

by Holly Ziegler Hagen

In *Make It Happen with Feng Shui*, the reader gets amazing power packed information on attracting what we want to bring into our lives. Jen Leong has done a marvelous job assembling easy to use methods based on Feng Shui principles to optimize the reader's overall well-being and success.

Each chapter that explains more about the Feng Shui "bagua" (the ancient energy template) is about attracting what you want in that area of your life using the ancient wisdom of Feng Shui, aromatherapy, crystals and removing self-sabotaging behavior. I found particularly useful the Feng Shui Enhancement Overview that organizes important categories needed for quick reference. This is an excellent source for combining the Five Elements, areas of the Feng Shui bagua, associated colors, chakra, musical note, plus the application of essential oils and use of crystals.

Using specific crystals and aromatherapy techniques, Jen explains her TLC Process™ that enhance clearing and healing the mind and body with "energy from within." Jen places special emphasis on "reprogramming"—positive affirmations that guide the reader to turn negative issues into positive ones with clear examples that are easy to adapt to your own situation.

In every chapter, Jen shares success stories on how people have used Feng Shui, aromatherapy, crystals and her TLC Process™, illustrating how they attracted what they want in life. Enhancing wellness is the underlying theme of the entire book. Jen brings all her recommendations together with the Make It Happen Process™ where all holistic methods are combined to accomplish the reader's goals for well-being and success. Her use of Feng Shui guidelines enhance and form the framework for her easy, yet powerful methods.

The Appendix section of *Make It Happen with Feng Shui* is especially valuable. The author includes in-depth information on essential oils, crystals, and a useful worksheet on implementing the Make It Happen Process™.

After a year of my own challenging issues, I have used several of Jen's methods and found them to be remarkably helpful. I encourage readers to put Jen Leong's techniques to use and be ready for life transformation!

Holly Ziegler Hagen, Author
Sell Your Home FASTER with Feng Shui
Buy Your Home SMARTER with Feng Shui

Acknowledgements

Thank you to my good friends, Dhara and Rahasya Poe, authors of *The 12 Spiritual Laws of Recovery* and *To Believe or Not to Beleive: the Social and Neurological Consequences of Belief Systems,* for constantly encouraging me to write a book integrating Feng Shui and holistic methods. I also thank my clients who supported and encouraged me to share my knowledge, training and experience with the world.

Special thanks to my first Feng Shui mentor, Terah Kathryn Collins, author of *The Western Guide to Feng Shui,* who inspired and supported me in writing this book and provided me with the foundation of Feng Shui through her school, the Western School of Feng Shui™, and for giving me permission to apply her ideas and concepts throughout this book.

To my other Feng Shui mentors, Dr. Richard Tan, Master Peter Leung, Yasha Jampolski, Holly Ziegler, Denise Linn and Evanna Maggiore who furthered my knowledge in Feng Shui. To my Holistic Health mentors, including Dr. Brian Garrett, Dr. Bob Marshall, Dr. Dale Schusterman, Dr. Dan Harper, Dr. Dee Hahn, Dr. James Durlacher, Dr. John Thie, and Dr. Valerie Morton, to whom I am eternally grateful for all their knowledge, wisdom and experiences they have shared with me.

To all my colleagues and friends, who supported me and contributed to this book, including Dr. Brian Garrett, Dr. Dan Harper, Dr. Marla Brucker, Dr. Carolyn Mein, Holly Ziegler, Jennifer Buergermeister, Dana Race, Katherine Ball, Dr. Judith Andrews, Dr. Lia Andrews, Amanda Collins, Seth Collins, Charlotte Stover, Becky Hanson and Liv Kellgren.

To all those who shared their successful experiences using the self-help techniques from my system which helped to ground and complete this book.

To Anita Edmondson, my friend, editor and graphic designer, who helped shape this book. Her creative ideas and talents helped make this book the beautiful work of art that it is.

And thank you especially to my husband, Michael, and our daughters, Brooke and Krystal, for their patience and support and for sharing their time through this whole adventure.

Introduction: About the Book

This book is a tool for change. Within these pages, you will find specific, practical natural methods and techniques that you can apply to attract what you want in life, including success, prosperity, romance, happiness, and more.

What makes this book unique? I have researched and brought together natural methods to attract what you want on four key levels into one system that promotes life-changing enhancements and well-being. I will share with you the secrets of ancient wisdom and how to use them in our modern world.

Who can benefit from this book? Everyone! It is designed for the layperson with little or no knowledge about Feng Shui or Holistic Health who wants to enhance the quality of their life, as well as for the seasoned Feng Shui Practitioner or Holistic Health Professional working with clients looking for positive changes. Whether a novice or a professional, you will find this book to be a valuable reference tool you will use time and time again.

For the Novice

For those of you new to Feng Shui and/or Holistic Methods, you will be introduced to holistic methods to attract what you want in life. Holistic methods include more than physical healing with alternatives such as herbs, supplements, acupuncture chiropractic and massage therapy. It also includes emotional clearing to remove self-sabotage, clearing your way to attract what you want in life. Holistic Health can also encompass Feng Shui principles and practices, which can heal your environment by working and adjusting the flow of energy within a space, optimizing your wellness and success potential.

For the Professional

For professionals in these fields, you will learn about alternative ways for a better life that perhaps you have never encountered before that can be added to your professional "tool box." This book is filled with comprehensive reference charts that encompass simple and powerful techniques to attract what you want.

I am passionate about what I do, and I truly believe in the power of Feng Shui and other natural holistic methods. I have included my own success story in the last chapter. Be sure to read it. I hope that you will find similar success in reaching your goal(s) as you apply the tools and techniques you will learn from this book to enhance your own life and well-being. Do it for yourself. Make it happen!

How to Use this Book

As a reference tool, this book can be used two different ways. First, you can read it in its entirety to build a solid foundation for an understanding of the practice of Feng Shui, and how it can be used to attract what you want. The other way to use this book is as a reference for a specific area in your life that you would like to enhance. Part I gives you the fundamentals and Part II puts all the methods together.

For example, if you want to focus on a particular area, read Part I. This will give you an overview of Feng Shui, Chakras (sha-kras), and other natural healing methods, including the TLC (Transformational Life Changing) Process™, Aromatherapy and Crystals. Then find the chapter in Part II that addresses your specific life issue and learn how to use the Make It Happen Process™ to enhance your quality of life.

You also can refer to the different charts throughout the book for a quick overview, then go to the chapter pertaining to the area of your life you would like to enhance.

You will find a chapter dedicated to each of the nine areas, or "guas," of your life. Each chapter discusses the attributes of that gua (i.e., Career, Relationships, etc.) and the natural methods you can use to enhance that area of your life.

For Further Information

You will find a glossary of terms in the back of the book, which includes benefits of the essential oils and crystals. In addition, there are a number of useful appendices, worksheets, and a list of recommended reading and other resources that you will find quite valuable.

In this book, you will learn the **Make It Happen Process**™, which incorporates natural holistic methods that work on different levels of attracting what you want and how you can apply them together for optimum change:

Clearing the Way

1. **Feng Shui**—*environmental* healing achieved by adjusting the flow of energy within the space around you to promote well-being and harmony.

2. **The TLC Process**™ (Transformational Life Changing Process)—This technique helps you align your goals by removing self-sabotage and affirming what you want to attract in life.

Setting Your Intentions

3. **Aromatherapy**—*biochemical* healing within the mind and body. The therapeutic power of essential oils can enhance a specific area in your home, health or life by helping you set your intentions to create new positive thought patterns.

4. **Crystals**—gemstones provide the *physical* anchor that facilitates life-changing success and well-being. By choosing the right crystals, you can focus and amplify positive energy needed for well-being and to set your intentions for attracting what you want.

Apply Now or Later, One or All

While not intended to be a comprehensive guide on Feng Shui or natural holistic methods, this book provides an introduction, or for some of you, a deeper understanding of some natural holistic methods and how you can use them together. You might also discover that some of the material in this book will become useful to you at a later time, although it may not seem applicable at the moment.

As a Feng Shui and Holistic Health Professional myself, I truly believe in a layered approach to addressing the depths and complexities of issues or concerns faced by clients. My combined experience over the past eighteen years as a Feng Shui and Holistic Health Practitioner has shown that you can achieve better and faster results by applying various holistic modalities to attract what we want in life.

Part I

Mastering the Fundamentals

The "Whys" & "Hows" of Feng Shui

Wind and Water

Feng Shui (*fung shway*) is Chinese for "wind (*Feng*) and water (*Shui*)." It is a philosophy based on common sense and observations about energetic influences on the environment that have been gathered by Chinese masters over thousands of years. The "wind and water" reference describes the flow and accumulation of energy or "chi" in our environment.

The concept of the energy flow of "wind and water" also applies to the home and office in regards to the proper placement of furniture, windows, doors, and other objects. Thus, we can use the principles and techniques of Feng Shui to bring balance and harmony into our home or office by changing the energy around us. The subtle yet powerful influence of energy has a profound effect on different aspects of our lives, such as health, happiness, prosperity and relationships.

Yesterday and Today

The art and practice of Feng Shui can be traced back more than 3,000 years to ancient China. Some sources even suggest that it has been in existence for at least 5,000 years. Historians have found records in Feng Shui text dating to the period of Confucius (551–479 B.C.). Although Feng Shui remained an unwritten practice for many centuries, there were an estimated 57 books on Feng Shui during the Sung Dynasty (A.D. 960–1129). It was also mentioned in folklores, poetry and medical texts.

In the early days, Feng Shui was reserved only for the Imperial Court and senior officials of the Chinese government; its tools and techniques kept secret from the common people. In fact, those who practiced it illicitly were sentenced to prison or death. The Chinese government even prohibited the practice of Feng Shui during the first 30 years of the communist reign from 1950–1980.

Feng Shui was used extensively by the Chinese to determine the most auspicious burial site for ancestors. It was thought that if the ancestors were pleased with their burial location, they would look after the living, ensuring that good fortune be bestowed upon them.

Chinese emperors also employed Feng Shui principles to determine the ideal location for their palaces. In time, this practice was adopted by the people of China to find the best locations for homes and business buildings. Today, it is common in the Chinese culture to have a Feng Shui consultation before buying a house or leasing a business office.

Feng Shui has literally traveled through space, time and evolution from the Far East to all corners of the world. Tools and techniques have changed to adapt to modern ideas and needs, particularly in the Western world, transforming Feng Shui into the art and practice as we know it today.

Creating a Positive Chi Flow

Feng Shui is based on how energy or "chi" moves through our environment, either in a positive or negative way. The principles and foundations of Feng Shui provide us with a method of working with the energetics of the home. The general rule of thumb is that the eyes tend to follow the direction of energy flow.

For example, when you enter a home that has a large picture window in the back directly across from the front door, you will automatically look straight out the backyard. This means the energy coming in the front door is flowing straight through the back door or window, along with wealth and health.

Another example is when you walk into a bathroom where the toilet lid is open. Your eyes will be drawn right to the toilet and then down the "drain." The energy is being drained out of the room going straight down the toilet, just like the saying "money (or health) going down the toilet."

The good news is that you can apply simple tools and techniques of Feng Shui to redirect and refine the energy flow, minimizing the negative effects created in situations like these. For example, the energy flowing down the toilet can be adjusted simply by closing the lid.

Three Foundational Principles of Feng Shui

There are three basic principles of Feng Shui. Simple, yet powerful, they can be applied immediately to your own environment to start bringing harmony and balance within and around you. These principles, and the three guidelines that follow, are adapted from *The Western Guide to Feng Shui* by Terah Kathryn Collins.

1. All Things are Alive.

We tend to think of humans, animals and plants as alive or living. However, inanimate objects are also alive in the sense that they elicit associations—positive or negative—in our conscious and subconscious mind. For example, a seashell you found on vacation might remind you of the happiness and good time you experienced. On the other hand, a picture of a lonely woman might serve only as a reminder to a single woman that she is still alone.

Here is a simple exercise you can do right now. Look around your environment (home or office). What are your belongings saying to you? Do they have positive associations, or are they saying negative things to you? Removing any items that have negative associations is one way to start creating a more harmonious environment around and within you.

2. All Things are Connected.

Whether we are aware of it or not, everything and everyone is connected energetically in some way. For example, poor health can have a negative effect on your prosperity and relationships. If you do not feel well, you do not have the energy to work and make money. This can cause stress or disharmony in your relationship with your spouse or significant other because money, especially a lack of it, is one of the most common sources of contention with couples.

However, if you are in good health, you are able to work and be prosperous. You have enough money to pay bills and even have some fun. This should help make your spouse or significant other happy and lead to a more harmonious relationship.

Of course, these are oversimplified examples, but you get the point. Once you understand how different areas of your life are connected, you can begin to make adjustments accordingly by using the appropriate Feng Shui techniques.

3. All Things Change.

You've heard the adage: the only thing that is constant is that everything is constantly changing. We, as people, and our environment are always in a state of flux—our careers, our families, our homes, and our personal preferences. It is important to make sure that our environment reflects who we are now.

For example, at one time you might have loved the color blue and incorporated it in your décor. Now, a completely different color resonates with you and reflects your growth in style or taste. Therefore, you should change the colors (or furniture, artwork, accessories, etc.) in your home to reflect the "new you." This will bring the outer Feng Shui of your home in harmony with the inner Feng Shui of your mind and body.

Three Practical Guidelines to Living a Better Life

The three principles previously discussed provide the foundation for the following guidelines to living a better and happier life. Like the principles, these three guidelines can help harmonize your outer Feng Shui with your inner Feng Shui. Harmony supports an environment for better well-being and to attract what you want.

1. Surround Yourself With What You Love.

Knowing that everything is alive with associations, you should now be aware of what your belongings, such as artwork and furniture, are saying to you. Living with what you love enhances your chi and can therefore enhance your well-being. Likewise, living with items that have negative associations can lower your chi, and subsequently your quality of well-being.

Take a look around your home and remove items that have negative associations. Then take away "neutral" items that elicit neither a positive nor negative feeling. Surround yourself with images or objects that you love, and that represent good health, such as healthy plants, luscious landscaping, even pets. These will also enhance the positive chi in your home.

REFLECTION

Imagine living only with what you truly love. Now imagine how this might raise your chi, thereby providing and supporting an environment for optimum well-being and success.

2. Surround Yourself With Comfort & Safety.

Ultimately, you want to create an environment that nurtures and protects your physical and mental well-being. Take a look around your home. Does your furniture have sharp corners? Do you have a coffee table or other item in the way of your home's high traffic areas? Do you have a bruise on your leg, hip or other part of your body from repeatedly running into furniture?

REFLECTION Imagine living with objects and furniture that are Feng Shui-friendly, comfortable and safe. Imagine how this could allow your subconscious mind to relax, thereby reducing stress and creating an environment for better well-being and success.

If you answered "yes" to any of these questions, your comfort and safety are being compromised. You are spending conscious and sub-conscious energy trying to avoid running into furniture. This puts extra stress on your body, which in turn, puts stress on your well-being. Move furniture, plants or other objects that present a physical challenge to a "safer" location.

Sharp corners also pose potential physical harm, as they are like "secret arrows" that emit negative chi. To dodge these arrows, avoid sitting or lying in line with any sharp corners of furniture, walls, or other physical structures. Whenever possible, select furniture with rounded corners for comfort, safety and harmony.

3. Get Organized & De-Clutter.

REFLECTION Did you ever notice how much better you feel after spring cleaning; clearing the closet of "expired" clothes; or cleaning out the junk drawer? It makes the air fresher and gives you room to breathe!

Ever wonder why you are unable to get any work done when you are facing a messy desk? Do you have difficulty finding an outfit to wear when your closet and/or bedroom is in disarray? Clutter and dust contain stagnant chi since there is no room for the energy to circulate. This stagnant chi provides a less than excellent environment for good health. Clearing clutter allows good chi to circulate and flow creating a healthier environment and bringing in auspicious opportunities. You are also eliminating the stale chi that was stored in those items removed. Keep your environment organized by de-cluttering on a continuous basis to allow new opportunities to come in your life.

The Bagua Map:
A Tool for Creating Success

To determine the energy flow of a home or business office, Feng Shui practitioners use the Bagua Map. Bagua literally means eight (ba) areas (gua), referring to the eight key aspects of life and the corresponding areas within the home or office. Keeping the energies balanced in all areas enhances unity, health and harmony to support an environment to attract what you want in life.

1. **Career**—where grounding, security, courage and confidence provide the foundation for success.

2. **Knowledge & Self-Cultivation**—where the environment for learning and spiritual growth can thrive. Other qualities associated with this area include intuition, wisdom, inner vision, awakening, stillness and self-cultivation.

3. **Family & Health**—where strength can assist in staying emotionally and physically balanced. Healthy relationships, minds and bodies lay the foundation for personal growth and happiness.

4. **Wealth & Prosperity**—where personal power and gratitude can enhance prosperity. Wealth & Prosperity is not limited to money. It also includes an abundance of all aspects of your life, such as health and happiness.

5. **Fame & Reputation**—where appreciation and recognition can enhance your reputation. Integrity of your actions also contributes to your reputation and can illuminate your life with the good will of friends, co-workers and the community.

6. **Relationships, Love & Marriage**—where you can enhance loving relationships. Here, receptivity is important in communication. Unconditional love and support, flexibility and adaptability and devotion are other qualities associated with this area.

7. **Creativity & Children**—where creativity and youthful joy can thrive. Encouragement, generosity and pleasure are also qualities associated with this area. When this area is enhanced, children and adults can learn and grow through creative expression.

8. **Helpful People & Travel**—where synchronicity (how all aspects of your life flow) and timing can enhance good fortune. When this area is enhanced and in harmony, all aspects of our life appear to flow easily and bring about good fortune. Inspiration, confidence and power are other qualities associated with this gua.

These eight areas revolve around the center of the home known as Tai Chi: Health & Unity:

9. **Tai Chi: Health & Unity**—where all aspects of your life come together. This is like the hub of a wheel that connects the eight areas of the Bagua Map.

REFLECTION

Regardless of which Feng Shui philosophy or bagua map is used, the ultimate goal is to achieve optimal results in health, happiness and harmony in all aspects of our lives.

Feng Shui Schools

Classical Feng Shui, also known as Traditional Feng Shui, is the original School that all other Feng Shui Schools have come from, including Form School and Compass School. Classical Feng Shui does not incorporate the bagua map. Instead, this school of thought uses the concept of time and space to the different compass directions to determine the quality of energy flow of that area of the home, office or building.

As Feng Shui developed over the years, two types of Bagua Maps emerged: Compass or Directional and Non-directional (Form).

The Compass (Directional) method is usually based on the direction the front door faces (North, South, etc.). This is used as a reference point to aligning the different guas of the home or office building. Other Feng Shui practitioners apply the Non-directional Bagua Map, which is based on the location of the front door, regardless of compass direction. Keep in mind that the Bagua Map is just a reference tool. One gua does not immediately stop and another begins. Rather, the energy flows from one area into the next.

This book includes both types of Bagua Maps to honor both philosophies. The guidelines that are explained and provided here can be applied to either the Compass or Non-directional Bagua Map. Over time, a number of other Feng Shui philosophies also have developed. For more information, see the Bibliography & Recommended Reading section of this book. Regardless of which philosophy or map is used, the ultimate goal is to create health, happiness and harmony in your environment.

For those who wish to use Classical Feng Shui, the natural holistic methods in the following chapters can still be applied to the time, space and direction to enhance the part of life you want.

Compass (Directional) Bagua Map

The Compass School of Feng Shui originated in the plains of China. Since there was no "form" such as mountains, hills, etc., direction was used. This philosophy is based on the idea that there is an optimal direction that a house should face based on the birth date(s) of those who live there.

A compass reading is taken at the entrance of the home or building facing the street most of the time. Some Feng Shui practitioners will take a reading from the entrance door even if it is not facing the street. Then, the center of the house is located and lines are drawn through this center point to the front entrance to determine the eight directions of the home or building (N, NW, W, SW, S, SE, E, NE).

THE BAGUA MAP
Compass

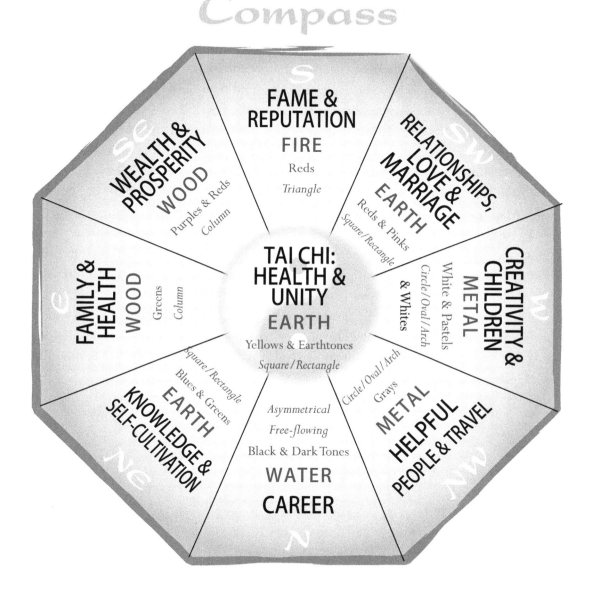

In the Compass School of Feng Shui, each gua (area of life) is associated with a different compass direction. To enhance a specific gua, you would apply Feng Shui remedies or techniques to the directional area in your home indicated on the Compass map. For example, if you wish to enhance your Wealth & Prosperity, you would focus on the South East area of your home; to enhance your Career, apply Feng Shui remedies to the North section of your home.

Non-directional Bagua Map

Today, most of us do not have the luxury of selecting the exact site to build our home. We choose a house that is already built, or an open lot that is available. In either case, we usually do not have the opportunity to determine the precise location or energy of the land, or the direction the house faces. For situations like these, the Non-directional Bagua Map may prove to be a more practical method than the Compass Map.

Although the Compass method can still be applied, some Feng Shui practitioners prefer to use the Non-directional Bagua Map. This system is based on a rectangle or square with nine equal areas (guas). This grid is then applied to the floorplan of the house or building, lined up with the front entrance of the home. (See picture on next page.) Unlike the Compass Bagua Map, the location of guas on the Non-directional Bagua Map remains constant, regardless of which direction the front door is facing.

There are some discrepancies amongst Feng Shui practitioners as to the location of the Health gua. Some experts believe that Health is central to everything and should be located in the center of the house, while others include it in the Family Gua (middle left gua or compass direction: East).

After researching the essential oils for the nine areas of the Bagua Map, I found that many of the same oils that cultivate health also support loving family relationships. Therefore, these Bagua Maps show Health with both the Family gua and the Tai Chi: Health & Unity gua.

THE BAGUA MAP
Non-Directional

WEALTH & PROSPERITY	FAME & REPUTATION	RELATIONSHIPS, LOVE & MARRIAGE
WOOD	FIRE	EARTH
Purples & Reds	Reds	Reds & Pinks
Column	*Triangle*	*Square / Rectangle*
FAMILY & HEALTH	**TAI CHI: HEALTH & UNITY**	**CREATIVITY & CHILDREN**
WOOD	EARTH	METAL
Greens	Yellows & Earthtones	White & Pastels
Column	*Square / Rectangle*	*Circle / Oval / Arch*
KNOWLEDGE & SELF-CULTIVATION	**CAREER**	**HELPFUL PEOPLE & TRAVEL**
EARTH	WATER	METAL
Blues & Greens	Black & Dark Tones	Grays
Square / Rectangle	*Asymmetrical / Free-flowing*	*Circle / Oval / Arch*

ENTRANCE

Align the entrance of your home or office with the above Non-Directional Bagua Map. To enhance a specific gua, you would apply Feng Shui remedies or techniques to that area in your home indicated on the Bagua Map. For example, if you wish to enhance your Wealth & Prosperity, you would focus on the far left corner of your home; to enhance your Career, apply Feng Shui remedies to the center front section of your home.

The 5 Elements:
A Balancing Act for Enhancing Your Life

There are five elements from nature that have been applied to traditional Oriental Medicine for better health and extended into Feng Shui. These include Water, Wood, Fire, Earth, and Metal. This book will focus on how each element is associated with an area of the Bagua Map. Therefore, including items that represent the element associated with a specific gua, may enhance that corresponding area of life.

Too much or too little of an element can have a profound effect on your mental, emotional and physical well-being. However, other elements can be applied to balance any extremes. For example, too much Water (i.e., bathroom or a leaking pipe or faucet) may cause respiratory problems. By adding the Earth element, you can "dam up" the excess water to lessen its effect, in the same way a beaver builds a dam to stop or slow down water.

The chart on the next page gives you a quick overview of the 5 Elements and how you can use them to enhance a specific gua or area in your life.

For example, if you have an issue with challenges reaching your Career goals. Take a look at the 5 Elements chart. This chart shows that Career is associated with the element of water and can be enhanced by adding items with the colors of black/dark tones, asymmetrical or free flowing shapes, and/or materials that are made of or represent water, such as fountains, ponds or reflective surfaces such as mirrors. Using one or more of these enhancements in the Career gua of your home may help you attract what you want in life.

Later in this book, you will learn in more detail about ways that you can use the color, shape and materials related to these elements to enhance specific aspects of your life. For a more complete understanding of how the five elements work together, take a look at the Feng Shui books listed on the Bibliography and Recommended Reading page at the back of this book.

THE 5 ELEMENTS
Enhance Your Life

ELEMENT	GUA	ENHANCE WITH:		
		COLOR	SHAPE	MATERIALS
WATER	Career (N)	Black Dark Tones	Asymmetrical Free-flowing	Water, Ponds, Fountains, Reflective Surfaces
WOOD	Family & Health (E)	Greens	Columnar	Wood, Plants, Flowers
FIRE	Fame & Reputation (S)	Reds	Triangle Pyramid Cone	Lighting, Animals, People
EARTH	Tai Chi: Health & Unity (Center)	Yellow Earthtones	Square Rectangle	Brick, Tile, Adobe, Ceramic Items
METAL	Creativity & Children (W)	White Pastels	Round Oval Arch	Metals, Rocks, Natural Crystals

The compass direction indicated under each gua name applies when using the Compass Bagua Map. Otherwise, use the gua location according to the Non-directional Bagua Map on page 11.

"He who lives in harmony with himself
lives in harmony with the universe."

— Marcus Aurelius

2 Success Begins at Home

Success on Many Levels

Our well-being affects our overall quality of life. Exercise, diet, sleep, relationships, and mental/emotional/spiritual well-being are all contributing factors. Our well-being in turn affects our success.

When we require healing at the physical level, we go to a health professional. For mental or emotional healing, we seek the advice of a psychologist or holistic health professional. We find spiritual healing with the help of a priest, pastor, rabbi or other religious/spiritual leader. What about healing on the environmental level? For that, we can look to the art and science of Feng Shui.

In the realm of Feng Shui, the term health can also be applied to the different aspects of life represented in the Bagua Map (see illustrations on pages 9 and 11). For example, do you have a healthy relationship with your spouse, children or family? Are your finances in good health? Are you enjoying a healthy rewarding career or job, one that lets you balance your work and home life?

If we lack wellness in one or more of these areas, our physical and mental health can suffer. Feng Shui enables us to adjust our environment to create harmony within and around us for optimum well-being.

REFLECTION

Are the different areas of your life in harmony and balance in a way that allows you to flow through life with ease and less stress to enhance your success?

How Form Affects Success in Your Life

There are two main schools of Feng Shui under classical Feng Shui—Compass and Form—upon which all other Feng Shui philosophies are based. The Compass School focuses on the direction the house is facing, while the Form School considers physical structures, objects and shapes around and within the house. Form also refers to the layout of the house, including location of doors, windows, stairs and bathrooms. These structures or forms can affect the chi or energy of the home. You will notice that "chi" and "energy" are used interchangeably.

Following are some of the major forms around and within your home that directly affect well-being, as well as tips on how to remedy the situation. Let us take a walk through some potential Feng Shui challenges, starting from outside the front of the home to the backyard.

Cul-de-sacs

In general, houses located in the keyhole, or end of cul-de-sacs are not optimum, especially the house directly at the end. Streets are like rivers where the energy flows, and once the energy reaches the end of the cul-de-sac, it has no place to go except directly at the house, much like a tidal wave. Too much chi coming directly at a home can be detrimental to the well-being of its residents.

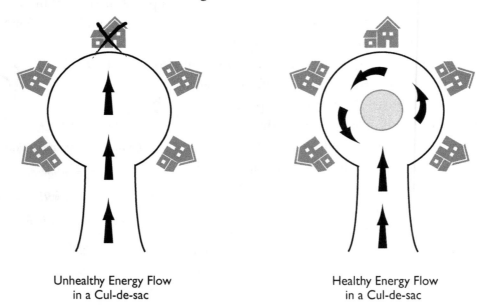

Unhealthy Energy Flow
in a Cul-de-sac

Healthy Energy Flow
in a Cul-de-sac

The chi can also stagnate within a cul-de-sac having no other place to go. However, a cement or green island in the middle of the cul-de-sac can help the chi circulate better.

Feng Shui Remedies:

- *Slow down the chi coming directly at the house by planting a hedge or putting up a small wall as a buffer between the street and your house.*

- *Place a bagua mirror above the front door or on the eave of the house facing the street with the intention of neutralizing the negative energy directed at your house. A bagua mirror is a special eight-sided Feng Shui mirror that neutralizes adverse energy.*

Front Door

The front entrance to your home should be clear of clutter, overgrown plants, or other objects. Having an open, easy access to the front door allows for auspicious (good, positive) chi to flow into the house. Blocked paths can hamper new opportunities and well-being.

Blocked Energy Flow   **Open Energy Flow**

If possible, avoid having the front door in direct line with any doors, sliding glass doors, or windows in the back of your house. When these are in alignment, energy flows in and then directly out the back. The same could be said for your health, wealth and other areas of your life. The objective is to keep energy flowing within your home.

Feng Shui Remedies:

- *Place a folding solid screen, bookcase or tall plant between the front door and back door / windows, if space allows.*

- *Hang a round, faceted Feng Shui crystal between the front door and the back door / window.*

- *If appropriate, do both.*

Stairs

Stairs facing or flowing towards the entrance to your home can negatively affect your health and wealth. Good chi cannot stay in the house because the energy goes down the stairs straight out the front. Incidentally, money and health go right out the door, too. A spiral staircase is particularly undesirable because it symbolizes a corkscrew that accelerates the movement of energy downward even more within your home.

Stairs located in the center, or heart of the home, can affect the cardiovascular system and the digestive system. The energy flow down the stairs is much like a roller coaster ride that gives you an uneasy feeling in your stomach as you are sent racing down a hill. Central stairs give you a similar feeling because it is not grounded with the center of the home. Remember, the center of the home is associated with the Earth element. Therefore, incorporating Earth elements here can help keep you feel more grounded and alleviate the "roller coaster effect."

Feng Shui Remedies:

- *Place a round, faceted Feng Shui crystal above the bottom stair to help lift and redirect the chi that would otherwise go out the door.*
- *Place something tall, such as a plant (real or silk) on either side of the stairs at the bottom to lift up the chi.*
- *Place an area rug (semicircle would be best) at the bottom of the stairs that differs in color to the carpet to slow down the chi flow.*
- *Paint the walls in that area an earthtone color, such as yellow or beige.*
- *Along the stairway wall, hang pictures evenly across to give the feeling of being grounded.*
- *Place an item on the landing to ground the energy. The bigger the landing, the bigger the objects should be, but remember to leave plenty of space to walk around the items.*

  Large landing: chair and table

  Medium landing: smaller table with ceramic item(s)

  Small landing: large crystal rock on the floor or tall ceramic vase with fresh plants or silk flowers

Bathrooms

Bathrooms naturally contain many Water elements, such as water and mirrors, as well as Metal elements, like white walls, tiles, sinks and plumbing fixtures. Metal "holds" water, therefore, enhances the Water element. Too much or too little of an element can have a profound effect on your mental, emotional and physical well-being, so you should take care to balance it with other elements.

Bathrooms located in the center of the house can have a negative influence on your well-being because the center represents the Tai Chi: Health & Unity gua. In addition, the center of the house is associated with the Earth element, and the Water elements of a bathroom located here can drown the Earth element, thereby dampening the grounding and stability needed in our lives.

As the place of elimination, bathrooms have a great influence on the condition of our health. They must be kept clean to represent good health. In addition, bathrooms can be beautiful, even though they are a place of elimination. You can create a rich and relaxing spa atmosphere in your bathroom with scented candles, sea sponges, towels and toiletries presented in a decorative basket.

REFLECTION

Although the bathroom might be considered "dirty" because of the purpose it serves, the elimination process itself is not bad. Think of it as cleansing the body, enabling us to let go of physical and emotional waste.

Feng Shui Remedies:

- *Place a round faceted Feng Shui crystal above the toilet or in the middle of a small bathroom.*

- *Keep the toilet lid down to prevent your health and wealth from "going down the drain."*

- *Close the bathroom door to keep good health in the house and to prevent bad chi from flowing into the rest of the house.*

- *Enhance the bathroom with Earth elements, such as earthtone paint, ceramic accessories and tile.*

- *Incorporate Wood elements in the room, such as wooden items, live or silk plants, pictures of nature and green accessories.*

- *Enhance with Fire elements, including candles and accessories in the red or purple color spectrum.*

- *Limit items with Metal elements, such as the color white, items made of metal and items that are round or oval.*

Plumbing and Water-Related Items

The relationship between placement of furniture and plumbing can also affect your well-being. For example, beds placed against walls with bathroom or kitchen plumbing can cause restless sleep as the water flows through the pipes. A lack of quality sleep can lead to compromised health. In addition, broken or leaky fixtures represent your health and wealth being drained away, which may affect the success in other areas of your life.

Feng Shui Remedies:

- *Fix all leaks and sources of damp areas immediately.*
- *Place beds along walls without pipes (for sinks, toilets or refrigerator with ice-maker).*

Position of Beds and Desks

Your bed or desk should be placed in a command or power position, preferably with your head and back to the wall, so that you have visual control over your environment. The "support" of a wall behind you provides a solid foundation for comfort and safety, which translates into optimal well-being, physically and financially. Without being able to see the door and having that back support, the chi moves around you in that empty space, causing a subconscious feeling that someone or something will "sneak up on you." A window on the wall behind you also will elicit that same uneasy feeling, so avoid that arrangement as well, if possible.

Position of Bed

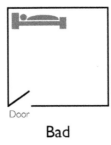
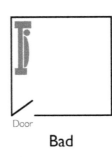
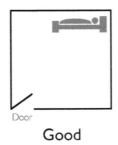

Door   **Bad**   Door   **Bad**   Door   **Good**   Door   **Good**

Feng Shui Remedies:

- *Position your bed and desk so that there is a solid wall behind you.*
- *If you cannot put your desk and chair in the command position, place a mirror on the wall in front, so you can see behind you, including the door.*
- *Place your bed away from walls against rooms with items that emit large amounts of EMFs (electromagnetic fields), such as a refrigerator, microwave, or stove in the kitchen; or computers, faxes, and printers in a home office. The harmful EMFs actually go straight through the wall.*

Plants

Houseplants that are vibrant and green represent good health. Likewise, sick plants represent poor health and literally can affect the well-being of the people living in that home. Dying leaves and flowers should be trimmed immediately to eliminate "dead" chi in the home. Avoid dried flowers and potpourri as they also represent dead chi.

Feng Shui Remedies:

- *Place a large, healthy plant in the Health gua of the home to represent good health. Silk plants are an acceptable substitution if you find it challenging to keep plants healthy, as long as they look vibrant and you keep them clean.*
- *Choose Feng Shui-friendly plants such as ficus, dieffenbachia and pothos, as well as any variety with rounded leaves. Avoid Feng Shui-unfriendly plants that have pointed leaves such as palms or cacti.*

Backyard

The shape of your backyard and the way it is arranged can also affect your well-being. Ideally, you want a mountain to provide protection for your home. However, many houses are positioned so that the open view is in the backyard. Often, this "view" is a canyon or a ledge that dramatically drops off. That drop off can cause the chi or energy flow to leave your property, along with your health, wealth and other areas of your life.

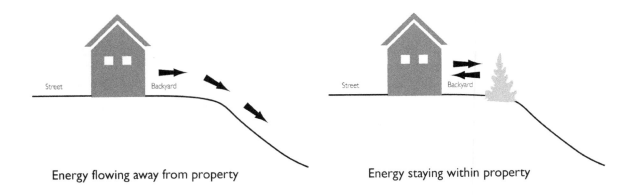

Energy flowing away from property   Energy staying within property

Feng Shui Remedies:

- *Plant tall trees in your backyard to provide the form of a mountain for protection and to keep the good chi on your property.*
- *Install a fence or wall along the back edge of your property.*
- *Place ceramic elephants with trunks up facing the house along the edge of the backyard along with the plants to anchor the yard and keep in the good chi.*

Offending Points

Sometimes items or forms on a neighbor's property can impact us. For example, your neighbor's roof corner, patio cover or decorative flagpole might point directly at your house. This sends secret arrows (negative chi) right at your house and can affect your well-being and/or prevent you from attracting what you want in life.

Feng Shui Remedies:

- *Place a wind chime between the offending points from the roof corner, patio cover or flagpole and your home to neutralize the secret arrows.*
- *Place a bagua mirror facing the offending roof corner, patio cover or flagpole with the intention of neutralizing the negative energy.*

Missing areas of the Bagua Map

When applying the Non-directional Bagua Map to your home, you might have missing areas because the shape of your home is not a square or rectangle. These areas must still be taken into consideration as they can affect the well-being of corresponding areas of your life, including relationships, prosperity, family and your health.

For example, if the Relationships, Love & Marriage area is missing, you might encounter challenges in your relationships. If the Wealth & Prosperity gua is missing, you could face financial difficulties. Missing areas in the Family and Health gua and, more rarely, the Tai Chi: Health & Unity gua, can cause major problems in health, as well as family matters.

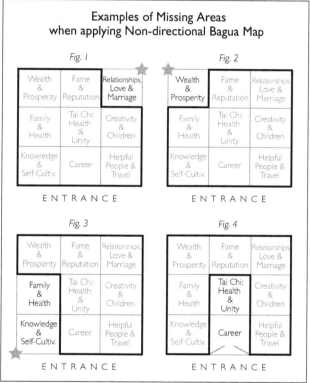

Examples of Missing Areas when applying Non-directional Bagua Map

Feng Shui Remedies:

Determine the exact corner of the missing area, by "squaring it" off (see stars on Figures 1-3). Then anchor the corner of the missing area with one or more of the following:

- *Fountain, if appropriate*

- *Flagpole or outdoor lamppost*

- *Statue appropriate for that area*

- *Fencing or hedges*

- *Tree proportionate to the size of the home. A two-story home would require a taller tree.*

- *Large boulder(s) with plants such as flowers or shrubs*

- *Any combination of the above*

For a U-shape house, such as Figure 4, install a fence with a gate to complete the gua(s).

Space Clearing

Your home or office may contain stagnant or less than excellent energy created by you and your family, or your home's previous owners/residents. Space clearing is a technique used to remove any stagnant or negative energy. We may experience less than excellent times in daily life, including arguments or negative thoughts, so it is beneficial to conduct space clearing on a regular basis. The result will be a more harmonious home/business environment. Space clearing relies on your mental intentions. You can say something like this as you do the clearing througout your space: "Clear all negative energies from this space and replace with white light on all levels now" and imagine that being done. What you project during the clearing is what you will create around you.

There are three main steps for a simple space clearing:

1. **Blessing**. Start with a blessing for the people of the house, and give thanks for what you have. Lighting a candle during the blessing is also very powerful as you set your intentions.

2. **Clearing-Purification.** There are several tools that can be used to clear your surroundings, including sound and sage. Regardless of which method is used, start at the front entrance and work your way clockwise, including every corner of your home or office with your mental intentions of clearing and/or blessing the space. You can also choose to open all the windows.

   • Sound vibration is a powerful way to clear unwanted energy, resulting in an immediate positive shift of energy. You can use bells, pots and pans, or even the clapping of your hands. Other more exotic sound-making devices are drums, tuning forks, gongs, singing bowls, and chimes.

   • Another common space clearing method is "smudging" with sage. Light a bundle of dried sage, then blow it out allowing the sage to continue smoking. You can keep the smoking sage in a bowl of sand to catch the ashes, as you move about to clear your space. Use your hand or feathers to fan the smoke. Another option is to use aromatherapy containing sage and other essential oils, if you don't like the smoke.

3. **Cleansing.** After your space clearing, cleanse all clearing tools with intention, sage and/or sound. Also, take a salt bath for approximately 20 minutes, using about 2 cups each of Epsom salt and sea salt to cleanse yourself.

"Life is a challenge, meet it!
Life is a dream, realize it!
Life is a game, play it!
Life is Love, enjoy it!"

— Sri Sathya Sai Baba

3 Chakras: The Energy Within & Around Ourselves

There exists yet another tool for achieving overall wellness and attracting what you want—the energy system. This system, like Feng Shui, harnesses the energy within and around us. It consists of 14 meridians and seven main chakras (sha-kras). Meridians are energy pathways, much like arteries and veins are pathways for the circulatory system. Acupuncturists insert needles along these meridians to either increase or decrease energy, which creates balance in a specific area of the body to improve health. These meridians work together in harmony with the body's chakra systems.

Chakra, a Sanskrit word meaning "wheel of light," is a vortex of whirling energy moving in a circular pattern that emanates from the front and back of the body. These energy centers regulate the energy flow and influence our response to situations and conditions in our lives.

The seven main chakras begin at the base of the spine and end at the top of the head. Each chakra has a specific purpose or "power" and is associated with different levels of consciousness and certain attributes. (See Chakra Overview chart on page 41.)

The first, second and third chakras, located from the mid-section down, are referred to as the "lower chakras." The fifth, sixth and seventh chakras, located from the throat up, are known as the "upper chakras." The fourth chakra, or Heart Chakra, bridges these two groups. The lower and upper chakras are equally important. Keep in mind that this is a system in which all chakras are intimately connected and communicating with each other.

Chakras for Success and Home

Chakras can be enhanced to achieve overall wellness and attracting what you want. Since each chakra is associated with an endocrine gland(s) in our body, we can tap into our body's energy system to enhance certain areas of our life and specific health issues. The "health" of each chakra—sometimes referred to metaphorically as being either closed (constricted) or too open (overblown)—reflects the state of health of your body and in the corresponding area of your life. For example, a sore throat or tight shoulders could reflect a constricted Throat Chakra. An enlarged, tight belly could suggest an overblown Solar Plexus Chakra.

In addition to the connection of chakras on the physical level, there is also a correlation with our emotional side. For instance, someone who has a difficult time giving or receiving love in a relationship might have a "closed" fourth chakra (Heart Chakra). An individual who has a hard time expressing his or herself might have a "closed" fifth chakra (Throat Chakra).

And lastly, chakras have a direct correlation to the guas of your home. Keeping in mind the basic Feng Shui principle that "all things are alive," we can consider our home to be a "living essence." When we apply the seven main chakras to the corresponding areas within the Bagua Map, we add another dimension to our ability to attract what we want in life. Later in this book, you will learn several ways to enhance chakra(s) associated with the different guas by using specific essential oils and crystals.

The 7 Chakras

Let us take a closer look at the seven main chakras of the energy system. Although there are two higher chakras (eighth and ninth) that exist above the head and other smaller minor chakras, this book will focus on the seven primary chakras. (See Bibliography and Recommended Reading section for more information on chakras.)

7 MAIN CHAKRAS

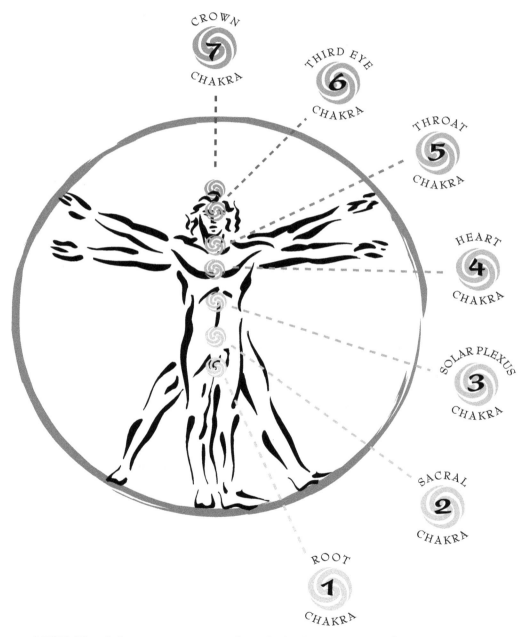

NOTE: The chakras emanate energy from the back as well as the front of the body.

1 ROOT (BASE) CHAKRA

The Root Chakra, also known as the Base Chakra, is located at the base of the spine and is associated with the color red. The Root Chakra is associated with survival and the tribal power of a group, which connects to family beliefs that support identity and the sense of belonging to a group of people in the same geographic area.

Level of Consciousness:

Associated with the physical realm and all physical sensations, including pain and pleasure.

Functions:

Provides the foundation and life force to the physical body. It also has to do with instinct, self-preservation and survival.

Qualities / Lessons:

Success and the material world. Qualities are grounding, stability, health and courage. The need for structure, order and logic are also associated with this chakra. It activates the will to survive, manifest and sustain life.

Working on this chakra can help with the following Emotional Challenges:

- Insecure, self-centered and angry.
- Overly concerned with survival.

Helpful People:

Those who provide traditional root relationships such as parents and grandparents help support the Root Chakra.

Feng Shui Guas:

The qualities listed above help support Career and Family & Health.

② SACRAL (SPLEEN) CHAKRA

The Sacral Chakra, also known as the Spleen Chakra, is located between the pubic bone and the navel and is associated with the color orange. This chakra is associated with emotions and sexuality and connects us to the power of relationships to satisfy physical and personal needs. The Sacral Chakra resonates to the flow of power between others and self.

Level of Consciousness:

Associated with the emotional realm, where all emotions are processed.

Functions:

Deals with reproduction, assimilation of food and vitality.

Qualities / Lessons:

Associated with emotions including desire, passion and pleasure. It governs creativity and sexuality. It has to do with the assimilation of new ideas, tolerance, surrender, and working harmoniously and creatively with others. It is also associated with health, family and the need for relationships.

Working on this chakra can help with the following Emotional Challenges:

- Confusion, lack of purpose, jealousy and envy.
- Sexual difficulties and desire to possess.
- Over-indulgence in sex and/or food.

Helpful People:

Those who teach us how to accept and share our feelings such as spouses and children help support this chakra.

Feng Shui Guas:

The qualities listed above help support Relationships, Love & Marriage, Creativity & Children and Family & Health.

③ SOLAR PLEXUS CHAKRA

The Solar Plexus Chakra is located between the navel and the bottom of the breastbone and is associated with the color yellow. This third chakra is connected to energy and personal power in relation to the external world.

Level of Consciousness:

Associated with the mental (intellectual) realm where thoughts, judgment and opinions originate and are controlled.

Functions:

Energizes the sympathetic nervous system and is associated with the digestive processes and metabolism of emotions.

Qualities / Lessons:

Associated with personal power, will, self-control, self-discipline, self-esteem, self-respect, mastery of desire, warmth/radiance, laughter and humor. It also has to do with our spiritual awakening and transformation.

Working on this chakra can help with the following Emotional Challenges:

- Anger, hate and fear.
- Over-emphasis on power and/or recognition.
- Taking in more than one can assimilate and utilize.
- Fear of rejection and criticism.

Helpful People:

Friends, classmates and intellectuals help support this chakra.

Feng Shui Guas:

The qualities listed above help support Wealth & Prosperity and Fame & Reputation.

HEART CHAKRA

The Heart Chakra is located at center of the chest and is associated with the color green. The secondary color is pink. This fourth chakra is connected to the power of emotion and how to express love and compassion with other people and situations.

Level of Consciousness:

Associated with the astral realm that connects the dimensions of matter and spirit. This is where transformation is made possible.

Functions:

Energizes the blood and physical body with the life force and is the connection to our emotional perceptions.

Qualities / Lessons:

Associated with unconditional love and possessing the ability to have compassion, understanding, acceptance, forgiveness and trust. The Heart Chakra is always working towards balance and harmony.

Working on this chakra can help with the following Emotional Challenges:
- Suppression of love, emotional instability and disharmony.
- Jealousy, hatred and inability to forgive.

Helpful People:

Spiritual teachers help support this chakra.

Feng Shui Guas:

The qualities listed above help support Relationships, Love & Marriage, Creativity & Children, Family & Health, Tai Chi: Health & Unity and Career.

⑤ THROAT CHAKRA

The Throat Chakra is located at the throat level and is associated with the color blue. This fifth chakra is associated with communication and creativity and the power of expressing will and choice.

Level of Consciousness:

Associated with the etheric realm, the first of the spiritual realm; also known as the light body that is the template for the perfect body.

Functions:

Connected with speech, sound, vibration and communication. It is also the connection to the emotional/mental struggles in the power of choice.

Qualities/Lessons:

Associated with communication, self-expression, personal authority, creative expression of speech, writing and the arts. It is also associated with integration, wisdom/knowledge, peace, loyalty, honesty, truth, reliability and kindness.

Working on this chakra can help with the following Emotional Challenges:

- Communication and speech problems.
- Ignorance, lack of judgment and unwise use of knowledge.

Helpful People:

Religious Leaders and Divine Rulers like the Pope and the Dalai Lama help support this chakra.

Feng Shui Guas:

The qualities listed above help support Helpful People & Travel and Creativity & Children.

THIRD EYE (BROW) CHAKRA

The Third Eye Chakra, also known as the Brow Chakra, is located just above and centered between the eyebrows and is associated with the color indigo (deep blue/purple). This sixth chakra is associated with intuition and imagination and connects us to the power of the mind, which involves our mental and reasoning abilities to evaluate our attitudes and beliefs. The Third Eye Chakra helps to bring wisdom through life's experiences and lessons.

Level of Consciousness:

Associated with the celestial realm, which stores each person's individual future and access to that future. It is the realm of sight, allowing us to "see the light."

Functions:

Energizes the lower brain (cerebellum) and central nervous system. It is also associated with vision.

Qualities / Lessons:

Connected to intuition, insight, inspiration, wisdom, imagination, dreams and visions. It is associated with concentration, calmness and physical manifestation of your thoughts and dreams.

Working on this chakra can help with the following Emotional Challenges:

- Lack of concentration, fear.
- Overly disconnected from the world.

Helpful People:

Spiritual teachers and friends help support this chakra.

Feng Shui Guas:

The qualities listed above help support Knowledge & Self-Cultivation and Helpful People & Travel.

CROWN CHAKRA

The Crown Chakra is located at the top of the head and is associated with the color violet. This seventh chakra is associated with divine wisdom and understanding and connects us to our spirituality. It gives us the ability to help our spirituality to become part of our physical lives.

Level of Consciousness:

Associated with the realm of pure consciousness, which stores our spiritual life. This is the cosmic link where we are connected with the Divine Source. This is where knowledge is beyond words.

Functions:

Energizes the upper brain (cerebrum).

Qualities/Lessons:

This chakra is also known as the "Seat of the Soul." It is associated with inspiration and timelessness and unifies the Higher Self with the human personality, divine wisdom/ understanding and selfless service.

Working on this chakra can help with the following Emotional Challenges:

- Lack of inspiration, confusion, depression and alienation.

Helpful People:

Prophets, gurus and saints help support this chakra.

Feng Shui Gua:

The qualities listed above help support Fame & Reputation and Wealth & Prosperity.

CHAKRA LOCATIONS
within the Bagua Map

WEALTH & PROSPERITY	FAME & REPUTATION	RELATIONSHIPS, LOVE & MARRIAGE
SOLAR PLEXUS Crown Heart	**CROWN** Solar Plexus	**HEART** Sacral
FAMILY & HEALTH	TAI CHI: HEALTH & UNITY	CREATIVITY & CHILDREN
HEART Root Sacral	**HEART** **SOLAR PLEXUS**	**SACRAL** Heart Throat
KNOWLEDGE & SELF-CULTIVATION	CAREER	HELPFUL PEOPLE & TRAVEL
THIRD EYE	**ROOT** Heart	**THROAT** Third Eye

Chakras shown in all caps are the primary chakra(s) for that gua. Others listed are supporting chakras that help to enhance that gua.

The chakras associated with each gua are the same on Compass (Directional) and Non-directional Bagua Maps (pg. 9 and 11).

Charting Our Chakra Course

To help us understand the many aspects of chakras and how we might use them to our advantage to enhance our lives and attract what we want, the Chakra Overview chart on the next page provides a synopsis of the various attributes of the seven main chakras:

Location: where the chakra is located on the body

Level of Consciousness: physical, mental, emotional, spiritual, etc.

Color: the color associated with that chakra

Sense: one of the five senses associated with each chakra

Feng Shui Gua: what areas of the home each chakra is associated with

REFLECTION

It is interesting to note that the Heart Chakra is at the center of both the body and the Bagua Map. It is also a supporting chakra in four other guas, appearing more than any other chakra.

CHAKRA OVERVIEW

CHAKRA	BODY LOCATION	LEVEL OF CONSCIOUSNESS	COLOR*	SENSE	FENG SHUI GUA**
1st ROOT (Base)	Base of Spine	Physical	Red	Smell	**Career** Family & Health
2nd SACRAL (Spleen)	Between the Pubic Bone & Navel	Emotional	Orange	Taste	**Creativity & Children** Relationships, Love & Marriage Family & Health
3rd SOLAR PLEXUS	Between the Navel & Bottom of Breastbone	Mental	Yellow	Sight	**Wealth & Prosperity** Fame & Reputation Tai Chi: Health & Unity
4th HEART	Center of Chest	Astral	Green	Touch	**Love & Marriage Tai Chi: Health & Unity Family & Health** Creativity & Children Wealth & Prosperity
5th THROAT	Throat	Etheric	Blue	Hearing	**Helpful People & Travel** Creativity & Children
6th THIRD EYE (Brow)	Just Above & Centered Between the Eyes	Celestial	Indigo	Beyond the Senses	**Knowledge & Self-Cultivation** Helpful People & Travel
7th CROWN	Top of Head	Ketheric	Violet	Beyond the Senses	**Fame & Reputation** Wealth & Prosperity

*The colors associated with the chakras can be remembered by this mnemonic: ROY G BIV. The colors are in ascending order from Red to Violet.

**Feng Shui Guas in bold are primary guas.*

Enhancing Our Chakras

The Chakra Enhancement chart on the opposite page provides an overview of natural methods for enhancing each chakra of the body in relation to the Feng Shui guas to attract what you want in life.

Musical Notes: Play the corresponding musical notes in the corresponding gua of your home to enhance your life goal(s) and over the body chakra to help clear that chakra for better function and health. The musical note can be played alone or within some music, such as meditation or chakra balancing music.

Essential Oils: Specific essential oils will enhance the emotional influence of the body and enhance life goals when applied to the chakras or the corresponding gua.

Crystals: Certain crystals will enhance the emotional influence and health of each chakra and anchor affirmations and life goals when placed in the corresponding gua.

CHAKRA ENHANCEMENTS

CHAKRA	MUSICAL NOTE	ESSENTIAL OILS	CRYSTALS
1st **ROOT** (Base)	C	Cypress, Pine, Spruce, Vetiver	Black stones, e.g. Black Tourmaline, Obsidian, Smoky Quartz Red stones, e.g. Garnet, Red Jasper, Ruby
2nd **SACRAL** (Spleen)	D	Lavender, Orange, Pine, Sandalwood, Ylang Ylang	Orange stones, e.g. Amber, Carnelian, Citrine
3rd **SOLAR PLEXUS**	E	Bergamot, Cypress, *Frankincense*, Ginger	Yellow/golden stones, e.g. Amber, Golden Citrine, Gold, Tiger Eye
4th **HEART**	F	Orange, Lavender, Rose, Sandalwood, Ylang Ylang	Green stones, e.g. Aventurine, Emerald, Green Tourmaline, Jade, Malachite Pink stones, e.g. Pink Tourmaline, Rhodocrosite, Rhodonite, Rose Quartz
5th **THROAT**	G	Lavender, Lemon, *Peppermint*, Pine	Blue stones, e.g. Amazonite, Aquamarine, Celestite, Chrysocolla, Lapis Lazuli, Sodalite, Turquoise
6th **THIRD EYE** (Brow)	A	Mental Clarity: *Juniper*, Lemon, *Peppermint*, Eucalyptus Meditation: *Frankincense, Myrrh*	Indigo stones, e.g. Azurite, Lapis Lazuli, Sodalite
7th **CROWN**	B	*Frankincense, Myrrh*, Sandalwood	Violet/purple stones, e.g. Amethyst, Purple Fluorite

CAUTION: Avoid essential oils in bold italic during pregnancy.

"You can do anything you wish to do, have anything you wish to have, be anything you wish to be."

—Robert Collier

4 The Make It Happen Process™: Attracting What You Want

In this chapter, you will learn how to apply three natural, holistic methods to the home and/or body to enhance the different areas of your life. These methods work on three different levels—mental/emotional/spiritual, biochemical and physical—to provide specific steps towards accomplishing your goal(s). This forms what I call the Feng Shui Success Triangle which, when applied together, is called the **Make It Happen Process™** and can attract what you want in life. It consists of:

1. **The TLC Process™**, or Transformational Life Changing Process, works on the mental-emotional-spiritual levels. This technique helps you align your goals by removing self-sabotage and affirming what you want to attract in life.

2. **Aromatherapy** is for biochemical healing wthin the body and mind. The therapeutic power of essential oils can enhance a specific area in your home, well-being or life by helping you create new positive thought patterns to attract what you want.

3. **Crystals** provide the physical anchor that facilittes life-changing successes and well-being. By choosing the right crystals, you can focus and amplify positive energy needed to help achieve your goals and attract what you want.

FENG SHUI SUCCESS TRIANGLE

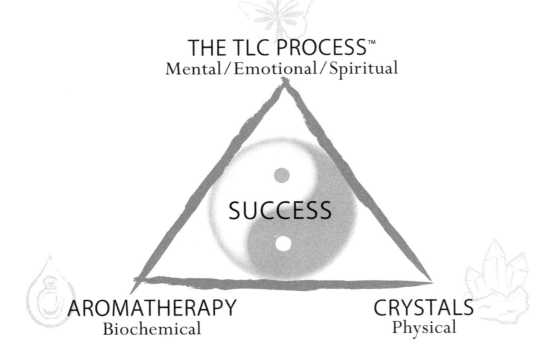

THE TLC PROCESS™
Mental/Emotional/Spiritual

SUCCESS

AROMATHERAPY
Biochemical

CRYSTALS
Physical

Through my many years of experience as a Holistic Health Professional, I have found that in most cases where there is a concern, the inability to achieve goals and change negative behavioral patterns stems from self-sabotage. Therefore, I have placed the TLC Process™ first to help clear the way for attracting what you want.

Aromatherapy and crystals are additional methods that aid in setting and anchoring your intentions on other levels in order to help you reach your goal(s). Together, integrating these three natural holistic methods are what I call the **Make It Happen Process**™.

The TLC Process™:
Clear the Mind, Attract What You Want

The TLC (Transformational Life Changing) Process™ is the first step in the Make It Happen Process™. It is a method of emotional clearing that I developed based on the premise that emotions are stored in our meridians (see Chapter 3) that "program" us to be the way we are, and that we can reprogram ourselves to attract what we want. It is similar to deleting an unwanted file on your computer and replacing it with a better updated version. In this way, the human body is a bio-computer that stores files that make us act the way we do. This falls in an area called Emotional Psychology.

There are a few forerunners of Emotional Psychology. John Diamond, M.D., used acupressure on the meridians to clear emotions. Later, Dr. Roger Callahan, a chiropractor, developed Thought Field Therapy (TFT). His method works on the body's energetic level to remove even fears and phobias. Gary Craig, the founder of Emotional Freedom Technique (EFT) also contributed to this field of Emotional Psychology. This method is also based on the connection between your body's subtle energies, your emotions, and your well-being.

The TLC Process™ is a step you can take toward achieving your goal(s). The entire process itself is beyond the scope of this book. However, I have extracted two simple, yet powerful steps from my TLC Process™ that anyone can do. This two-part process involves removing any self-sabotage or "emotional blocks" that prevent you from achieving success and then replacing them with positive affirmations. Adapted from Dr. Callahan's and Gary Craig's work, these steps help remove self-sabotage through deprogramming (step 1) and align you with your goal(s) by reprogramming with a positive affirmation of what you desire (step 2).

This method works by tapping certain points (associated with a meridian) on your hand as you repeat the deprogramming and reprogramming statements in each step to eliminate negative thought patterns and reprogram with positive thought patterns. An example of a deprogramming statement might be: "*I deeply accept, love and honor myself, even though…*" Examples of positive affirmations: "*I am successful in my career on all levels now*" or "*I deserve to be healthy on all levels now.*" I added "*on all levels now*" to this technique allowing for a more complete clearing.

While it might seem simple at first glance, the power of the mind and repetition used in both steps can produce faster and stronger results. Energy follows thought or intention. If you fill your thoughts or intentions with feeling, you may experience faster and stronger results.

STEP 1: Deprogramming (Clearing):

First, size up your current situation. Do you lack a close relationship with your spouse? Are you experiencing trouble advancing in your career? Do you have chronic problems? In other words, what area of your life do you want to improve?

Now, hold your left hand up toward your body, and with the fingertips of your right hand, gently tap on the side of your left hand below your pinkie finger (where your small intestine meridian lies), while repeating your deprogramming statement three times to clear your self-sabotage:

Examples of deprogramming statements:

"I deeply accept, love and honor myself even though I lack the ability to attract and have abundance in my life."

"I deeply accept, love and honor myself even though I feel stuck in my career."

"I deeply accept, love and honor myself even though I attract the wrong partner."

Saying *"I deeply accept, love and honor myself"* allows for change. Avoid using words in your statement, such as "not" and "don't," if possible, since these words are less empowering.

This step deprograms and clears your negative beliefs allowing you to move forward in a positive way.

STEP 2: Reprogramming (Affirmation):

Now, replace your deprogramming statement with a positive affirmation. Decide specifically what you want to accomplish. Do you want to receive recognition at work? Do you want to have a close loving relationship? Do you want to feel better physically?

Turn that goal into a positive affirmation and write it down on a piece of paper. Always add "on all levels now" at the end of your affirmation. This tells your mind and body to do it now! "On all levels" includes:

- Core level (programming from our childhood, usually the first 5 years)
- Genetic or historical level
- Karmic level (cause and effect)
- Levels or dimensions unknown at this time

Loosely hold your left hand palm down in front of your body. With the fingertips of your right hand, gently tap on top of the left hand in the groove between fourth and fifth knuckles (brain balance point on the triple warmer meridian) while repeating your affirmation statement three time with feeling.

Examples of reprogramming statements:

"I welcome and accept a steady flow of abundance on all levels now."

"I deserve to have a rewarding career on all levels now."

"It is good for me to have a healthy and intimate relationship on all levels now."

Do this step at least three times a day for one week to ensure that the new programming/alignment stays. Then follow up with the affirmation/tapping step as needed. You can also do the affirmation step any time you feel the need for more reinforcement. It is not necessary to repeat the deprogramming step after you have done it once, unless you feel a strong desire to clear again. No harm in doing so!

Aromatherapy: Sense the Changes from Within

Aromatherapy is the next step in the Make It Happen Process™ that works on the biochemical level and can be applied to Feng Shui. It is the use of the unique scent of essential oils for therapeutic or healing purposes.

Essential oils are concentrated plant essences extracted from the oil glands found in plant material such as leaves, flowers, root, bark, seeds, wood and resin. This oil is the lifeblood of plants and is the essence that gives off the distinctive aroma of each plant.

Pure essential oils can be quite expensive because of the extraction process and the number of plants required. For example, it takes:

- 2 tons (4000 lbs.) of rose petals to produce 1 lb. of rose oil

- 100 lbs. of French Lavender plant material to produce 1 lb. of lavender oil

One hundred percent pure essential oils are very concentrated. It takes only a few drops to produce a significant effect. The aroma can have a very powerful effect on our mind and body, as well as our environment.

Ancient Egyptians were among the first to create and use essential oils. They used myrrh as a natural fixative and cedarwood for anti-bacterial and antiseptic purposes when embalming and mummifying the deceased. Essential oils have also been used for thousands of years in incense, perfumes, cosmetics, and for medicinal purposes throughout India and China. The Tibetan temples also used frankincense and juniper for purification of the environment and body.

Characteristics of Essential Oils

Essential oils are not really oily at all. If left to evaporate, there would be no residue, except for the color. The consistency ranges from viscous to fairly solid. However, most essential oils, such as lemon, lavender and eucalyptus, are watery. The more viscous or resinous oils include frankincense, myrrh, sandalwood and vetiver. Essential oils also range in color—carrot is orange, spikenard is green, and chamomile is deep blue—however, most are usually clear.

How Essential Oils Work

There are two ways essential oils can enter the body:

Nose: The sense of smell is directly linked to the limbic brain where emotions, memory and regulatory functions of the body area located. This is the reason why smelling a certain scent can stimulate a memory.

Skin: The essential oil is absorbed through the pores and hair follicles of the skin to the capillaries and surrounding tissues (organs, muscles, etc.). The oils can be circulated throughout the body in as fast as 20 seconds.

Buying, Storing and Maintaining Essential Oils

To receive the maximum benefit of aromatherapy oils, it is essential to select quality oils and maintain them properly.

- Look for 100% pure essential oils with:

  Dark color glass bottles with dropper tops rather than eye droppers, which allow for greater evaporation.

  Latin names on the label or order form for single oils. For example, the Latin name for Bulgarian lavender is *Lavendula angustifolia*; Latin for peppermint is *Menthe piperita*.

- Store colored glass bottles out of heat and direct sunlight.

- Replace lid immediately to prevent evaporation and oxidation.

- Avoid flammable environments.

- For essential oils blended with carrier oils, add pure vitamin E (200–400 IU) per 2 ounces of carrier oil or jojoba oil (20%) as a natural preservative to prevent oxidation.

Using Essential Oils to Create a Healthier Home

Most essential oils are anti-bacterial, anti-viral, and some are even anti-fungal. Using aromatherapy in the home can literally create a healthier environment. Here are some easy ways to apply essential oils around your home:

- *Lamp Ring Diffuser:* Put 5–10 drops of oil into ring channel and place on light bulb. When the lamp is turned on, the warmth of the bulb will stimulate oils and subtly fill the space will a pleasant aroma.

- *Tealight Candle Diffuser* (aroma lamp): Fill "cup" with water. Add 10–20 drops of oil to water. Light candle and enjoy the healing scent.

- *Clay Pot Diffuser:* Put 15–30 drops of oil in pot. You can put a few drops on a cotton ball or piece of tissue. Good for small places like the bathroom, closet or even the car.

- *Air Freshener:* Use 30–40 drops of oil per 2 ounces of distilled water in a clean glass spray bottle, preferably colored. Try orange, lemon, peppermint or your favorite scent.

- *Natural Disinfectant:* Put 40–50 drops of tea tree and lemon oil in eight ounces of water. Use to clean countertops, flooring, kitchen and bathroom fixtures and appliances. Orange and grapefruit are also natural disinfectants.

- *Vacuum Enhancer:* Put a few drops of lavender or citrus oil on the filter of your vacuum cleaner or on a tissue in the vacuum filter bag. As you run the vacuum cleaner, the aroma will spread throughout the room. As an added benefit, this also neutralizes dust mites.

- *Laundry Boost:* Put a few drops of lavender or tea tree oil on a tissue for germ-free, fresh-scented laundry.

Applying Aromatherapy to Feng Shui for Life Enhancements

Aromatherapy can also be applied to Feng Shui to attract what you want. The fragrant influence of essential oils can be used to enhance the different guas to help achieve our goals.

For example, you can make a "gua spray" with a blend of distilled water and essential oils of rose and ylang ylang to enhance the Relationships, Love & Marriage gua of your home. Shake well and spray in all four corners and the center of the appropriate area of the home with intention of your affirmation and desired goal.

You also can use a body oil made from the same blend of oils above in a carrier oil, such as jojoba, and apply it to your Heart and Sacral Chakras to enhance Relationships, Love & Marriage. See the Feng Shui Enhancement Overview chart (pages 72–73) for more information.

Crystals: Anchor your Life Goals

Crystals are the next step in the Make It Happen Process™ that anchor your life-changing goals. Crystals are minerals made of silicon and oxygen (silicone dioxide), which scientists consider to be the building blocks of minerals, naturally embedded in clay. Each type of crystal has its own frequency of energy it emits or vibrates giving the crystal its unique color. The inclusion of other minerals in the same growth space as a crystal will alter the energy to a higher level and vibrational state. For example, the energy of:

- Amethyst is calming, emotionally balancing and enhances spiritual growth.

- Rose quartz enhances love, compassion and emotional healing.

- Clear quartz crystal has the capacity to absorb and reflect all color vibrations of the light spectrum.

One of the most common types of crystals is the clear quartz. These crystals have been used for healing, meditation and spiritual development by ancient civilization from around the world, including Native Americans, Aztec and Mayan Indians, Australian Aborigines, African tribes, Celts, Scots, Romans and the Ancient Egyptians. For example, religious figures used these crystals for healing, protection and to neutralize negative energy.

Other types of quartz crystals include amethyst, citrine and rose quartz. They, too, have been used for their natural powers including healing, meditation, technology and cleansing (purification). Crystals can also help you attract what you want. In general, they amplify energy and thoughts, both positive and negative, so be careful what you wish for!

Uses and Applications of Crystals

- *Healing*: Crystals conduct magnetic energy in a healing form.

- *Meditation*: For example, amethyst or blue lace agate is known to enhance the meditative state in the quest for transformation to higher consciousness.

- *Technology*: Crystals are used as part of circuits in televisions, radios and watches.

- *Manifestation*: On a metaphysical level, crystals can be personalized to help establish and reach your goals.

TYPES OF CRYSTALS

Single points:

- **Uses:** Meditation, healing, cleansing and linking energy.

- **Feng Shui Gua:** Where you need focus, such as Career, Knowledge & Self-Cultivation and Fame & Reputation.

Double terminated:

- To draw in, hold and release energy from both ends.

- Same uses as single points.

Clusters:

- At least two crystals that share a common base.

- Each crystal has its own frequency of vibration (energy) yet in harmony with each other.

- Energy is transmitted sporadically with the points constantly recharging each other.

- **Uses:** Meditation, healing, clearing negative energies and feelings.

- **Feng Shui Guas:** Where you want an abundance of something such as Wealth & Prosperity, Family & Health and Helpful People & Travel.

Nuggets / Tumbled Stones / Chunks:

- Broken off from larger crystals or clusters.

- **Uses:** Meditation and elixirs.

- **Feng Shui Gua:** Small tumble stones to represent Creativity & Children.
Use a pair of heart shape stones for Relationships, Love & Marriage.
Also can be used for any of the other Feng Shui Guas.

Crystal Balls (Spheres):

- Should be cut from chunks not from terminated crystals.

- Energy radiates from all sides.

- Magnifies your own energy back to you.

- **Uses:** Meditation.

- **Feng Shui Gua:** Tai Chi: Health & Unity; also can be used for any of the
other Feng Shui Guas.

Natural vs. Polished:

- Natural: The natural vibration of the crystal is not altered.

- Polished: Thought to increase storage capacity, more expensive.

Selecting a Crystal

- Which one are you drawn to?

- Do you have trouble putting it back down?

- Does it feel good to you?

- Do you just have to have it?

Cleansing & Clearing Crystals

Occasionally, crystals need to be cleansed and cleared of any negative energies from
emotional issues or previous owners. Do this by:

- "Smudging" with sage and positive thoughts, energy and white light.
See page 26 for more information on smudging.

- Place a clay mask (powder and water) around the crystal until at least dry. The negative energy and impurities are drawn out during the drying process. This is much like the spa treatment of a clay body wrap to help to draw out toxins from the body.

- Run under lukewarm water or stream while twirling the crystal (point up) back & forth while thinking positive thoughts, energy and white light.

- Soak in sea water or sea salt water (1c sea salt/1qt. warm water to dissolve) for a few to 24 hours or at least overnight (during full moon is best) in a non-metal container. Avoid this method for water soluble and 'soft' crystals.

  Make sure salt water solution is about the same temperature as the crystal(s) before placing them in the solution. Run under cool water to activate the energy flow once again after soaking.

Charging or Energizing Crystals

It is a good idea to recharge or energize crystals occasionally to restore their original strength or power of healing. This can be done after or during use, whether it is for healing the body or personalizing it to enhance your goals.

- Place cleared crystal(s) on a quartz crystal cluster.

- Place crystal on something natural (grass) in the sun for two to three hours or under the full moon for 24 hours. Avoid putting colored quartz in full sun or the color will fade.

- Imagine white light around and within the crystal.

Precautions

- Avoid placement of crystals on magnetic surfaces (personalized information may be erased).

- Avoid touching other people's crystals without permission, because of the transfer of your energy.

- Avoid exposure of crystals to rapid and extreme temperature changes since they are poor conductors of heat or cold.

- Avoid leaving colored crystals out in the sun for too long, especially amethyst (iron is unstable and the purple could fade).

- Avoid going near your crystals when you are angry or depressed. It will only amplify that energy back to you. If so, clear the crystals of the negative energy and replace it with white light and love.

Incorporating Crystals and Feng Shui for Life Enhancements

By combining two time-honored powerful healing approaches—Feng Shui and crystal therapy—you can create amazing results within and around you. It is surprisingly easy to incorporate crystals into Feng Shui using a Bagua Map of your home. You can place appropriate crystals in the various guas of the home for the desired enhancement. Crystals make beautiful decorative accessories. Place them directly on tables, mantles, countertops, in planters, as hanging art and so on. Be creative!

Personalizing the Crystal with your Affirmation

For greater impact, you can personalize the crystal with your positive affirmation for a specific Feng Shui area before placing it there. To personalize your crystal, follow these steps:

1. Hold the crystal in your left hand which receives energy.
   You can also hold it between your hands if the crystal is too big.

2. Place your right hand over the crystal which sends energy.

3. Say out loud or to yourself:

   "This crystal is personalized to (insert your affirmation here)
   on all levels now."

4. Focus your intent clearly into the crystal.

5. Imagine *and feel* yourself achieving the goals and results you want.

6. Say "Thank you. It is done, it is done, it is done."

Once the appropriate crystal(s) have been selected, cleared and personalized, place them in the Feng Shui gua you want to enhance. For example, if you want to enhance love and compassion with your significant other, place rose quartz in the Relationships, Love & Marriage area of your home. The following chapter includes more details and examples of how you can incorporate crystals to enhance your well-being and home.

CRYSTALS
to Enhance Feng Shui Guas

GUA	TYPE	COLOR
Career	Single points, tumbled stones, spheres	Black
Knowledge & Self-Cultivation	Points for focus	Blues Greens
Family & Health	Cluster, tumbled stones, sphere to bring in harmony	Greens
Wealth & Prosperity	Cluster or 8 tumbled stones to bring an abundance of prosperity	Purples Reds
Fame & Reputation	Single point for focus, tumbled stones, sphere	Reds
Relationships, Love & Marriage	A pair of heart-shaped stones or tumbled stones	Reds Pinks
Creativity & Children	Tumbled stones, sphere	White Pastels
Helpful People & Travel	Cluster, tumbled stones, sphere	Grays
Tai Chi: Health & Unity	Sphere to radiate energy from all "sides;" cluster to unite all areas of life	Yellow Earthtones

Make It Happen Process™—Putting it All Together

As mentioned in the beginning of this chapter, you can attract what you want using these three natural holistic healing methods that work on different levels of healing. With the Make It Happen Process™, you apply all three methods for a more powerful impact to accomplish your specific goal(s):

1. **TLC Process**™ for Mental/Emotional/Spiritual healing

2. **Aromatherapy** for Biochemical healing within the mind and body

3. **Crystals** for the Physical anchor that facilitates life-changing successes and well-being

Clearing the Way

STEP 1: THE TLC PROCESS™

Deprogram the negative, reprogram the positive

Addressing mental/emotional/spiritual healing is the first step toward achieving your goal(s). It is always best to remove any self-sabotage or "emotional blocks" and replace them with positive affirmations to better align yourself with your goals. I call this deprogramming your negative beliefs and reprogramming your positive beliefs. This simple, yet powerful, process can produce faster and stronger results.

Deprogramming (Clearing):

Hold your left hand up toward your body, and with the fingertips of your right hand, gently tap on the side of your left hand below your pinkie finger (where your small intestine meridian lies) while repeating your clearing statement three times:

> *"I deeply accept, love and honor myself even though I . . .*
> *(e.g. lack a healthy and intimate relationship in my life)."*

Avoid using words in your statement, such as "not" and "don't," if possible since these words are less empowering.

Reprogramming (Affirmation):

Loosely hold your left hand palm down in front of your body. With the fingertips of your right hand, gently tap on top of the left hand in the groove between fourth and fifth knuckles (where the brain balance point on the triple warmer meridian is located) while repeating your affirmation statement three times:

"I (e.g. attract and have a healthy intimate relationship)
on all levels now."

Do this affirmation step at least three times a day for one week to ensure that the new programming/alignment is anchored. Then follow up as you feel necessary.

Setting Your Intentions

STEP 2: AROMATHERAPY

Applying essential oils to the appropriate area of the home

Aromatherapy addresses healing on the biochemical level through the mind and body. First, select the appropriate essential oil(s) recommended to enhance a specific gua or area of your life. See chart on pages 72–73. Then apply as desired:

- **Around You:** Spray in all four corners and the center of the appropriate area of the home with intention of desired goal and affirmation. See the Aromatherapy section in this chapter for additional ways to apply aromatherapy around your home.

- **On Your Body:** Place one drop of the essential oil blend on your wrist, and rub your opposite wrist clockwise three times to activate and increase the frequency and power of the oils. Then use one wrist to apply the essential oil to the appropriate chakra on your body, moving your wrist clockwise three times with the mental intention of your desired goal and affirmation. Use the other wrist to apply the oil to any other chakras as needed.

  Do not worry if you rub in the "wrong" direction or forget which way to go. The main objective is to apply the oils to your body. Moving your wrist clockwise three times simply makes the application and intention a little stronger.

STEP 3: CRYSTAL THERAPY

Personalizing and placing crystals in the proper gua

Achieving life and wellness goals can be accelerated with the use of crystals or gemstones. For best results, write down your affirmation on a piece of paper, personalize your crystal and place it on the top of your written affirmation in the appropriate gua of your home as needed.

Personalizing your crystal:

1. Hold the crystal in your left hand which receives energy. You can also hold it between your hands if the crystal is too big.

2. Place your right hand over the crystal which sends energy.

3. Say out loud or to yourself:

    "This crystal is personalized to (insert your affirmation here) on all levels now."

4. Focus your intent clearly into the crystal.

5. Imagine and feel yourself achieving the goals and results you want.

6. Say "Thank you. It is done, it is done, it is done."

    Now place your personalized crystal over your written affirmation in the appropriate area of the home to anchor your goal. Success should soon follow!

A Case in Point

To understand how the Make It Happen Process™ works, and how you can apply it in your own life, let us take a look at a typical example:

THE SITUATION:

Joe is a successful, friendly and healthy man in his thirties. However, lately he has had trouble maintaining a romantic relationship. He has plenty of dates, but none of them blossom into a deeper romance. This, of course, is associated with the Feng Shui gua of Relationships, Love & Marriage.

STEP 1: TLC PROCESS™

Deprogram the negative, reprogram the positive

Now that Joe has identified the area in his life he wants to improve, he can develop a positive affirmation and use it to deprogram his negative beliefs and reprogram his positive beliefs.

> **DEPROGRAM:** Joe cleared any self-sabotage by tapping on the side of his hand while repeating the following statement three times (see page 50):
>
> *"I deeply accept, love and honor myself even though I lack a healthy and intimate relationship."*
>
> **REPROGRAM:** He then reprogrammed his positive beliefs by tapping on the back of his hand while repeating his affirmation statement three times: (see page 51).
>
> *"I attract and have a healthy and intimate relationship on all levels now."*

STEP 2: AROMATHERAPY

Applying essential oils to the appropriate gua and chakra(s)

In this step, Joe selects the appropriate essential oils for the chakra(s) associated with Relationships, Love & Marriage part of the home and body. (See chart on page 73.)

SELECTING THE OIL: Joe chooses a combination of rose, ylang ylang and other essential oils mixed with distilled water for a room spray. He also selects a body oil with the same blend that includes a carrier oil such as grapeseed and jojoba oil.

APPLYING TO THE GUA: While saying or thinking his affirmation—*"I attract and have a healthy and intimate relationship on all levels now"*—Joe applies the room spray to the four corners and the center of the Relationships, Love & Marriage area of his home.

APPLYING TO THE CHAKRA(S): Joe also places one drop of the body oil on his wrist and applies the body oil to his Heart and Sacral Chakras using a clockwise circular motion three times with the above intention.

STEP 3: CRYSTAL THERAPY

Personalizing and placing crystals in their proper place

To complete the process, Joe selects a crystal that is appropriate for the Relationships, Love & Marriage gua of his home. (See chart on page 73.)

SELECTING A CRYSTAL: Joe chooses a rose quartz crystal to enhance the Relationships, Love & Marriage area and to heal matters of the heart both emotionally and physically.

PERSONALIZING THE CRYSTAL: Using his positive affirmation, Joe personalizes the crystal to attract a healthy intimate relationship on all levels now. He imagines himself in the rose quartz being in a healthy intimate relationship. Joe then places the personalized rose quartz on top of his written affirmation in this gua of his home.

For real life success stories inspired by the Make It Happen Process™, read the chapters in Part II that address the key areas of life.

Enhancement At-A-Glance

The chart on the opposite page provides a summary of the attributes of the nine Feng Shui guas discussed in this section and how they relate to each other. You can use it as a quick reference to determine which Feng Shui attributes you can incorporate to enhance a specific area of your life.

For example, if you are having challenges in your relationship with your significant other, find the Relationships, Love & Marriage gua on the chart, then take a look across the row to see if the attributes listed are sufficiently present in that area of your home. If something is missing, adjust your decor to include those attributes. Also refer to pages 72–73 for further enhancements.

FENG SHUI GUAS
Attributes for Enhancement

GUA	ELEMENT	COLOR	QUALITY	CHAKRA
Career (N)	Water	Black	Courage	**Root** Heart
Knowledge & Self-Cultivation (NE)	*Earth*	Blues Greens	Stillness	**Third Eye**
Family & Health (E)	Wood	Greens	Strength	**Heart** Root Sacral
Wealth & Prosperity (SE)	*Wood*	Purples Reds	Gratitude	**Solar Plexus** Crown Heart
Fame & Reputation (S)	Fire	Reds	Integrity	**Crown** Solar Plexus
Relationships, Love & Marriage (SW)	*Earth*	Reds Pinks	Receptivity	**Heart** Sacral
Creativity & Children (W)	Metal	White Pastels	Joy	**Sacral** Heart Throat
Helpful People & Travel (NW)	*Metal*	Grays	Synchronicity	**Throat** Third Eye
Tai Chi: Health & Unity (Center)	Earth	Yellow Earthtones	Unity	**Solar Plexus** Heart

The direction indicated under the gua names apply when using the Compass Bagua Map. Otherwise, use the gua location according to the Non-directional Bagua Map on page 11.

Chakras in bold are primary for that Feng Shui gua. Elements in italics are included in the Compass Bagua Map.

Part II
Putting the Natural Methods to Work

Putting the Natural Methods to Work

The chapters in this section are organized by guas, starting with Career and ending with the center of the home, Tai Chi: Health & Unity. You will see a description of the gua, followed by the attributes and Feng Shui enhancements associated with it. You will discover how to apply the three natural holistic methods for each gua, including the TLC Process™ to remove self-sabotage (mental/emotional/spiritual), Aromatherapy (biochemical) and Crystals (physical) to anchor your intentions to attract what you want.

The Feng Shui Enhancement Overview chart on the following two pages serves as a handy reference for all guas, their attributes and applicable tools that you can use to enhance specific areas of your life to attract what you want.

To apply the information on this chart to your own life, find the area you want to enhance, then take a look at the attributes and holistic methods across the row. By incorporating one or more of these into the target gua, you may increase your chance of attracting what you want in that aspect of your life. Be sure to refer to the accompanying gua chapter in this section for more details on these natural holistic methods that can further enhance your success.

FENG SHUI ENHANCEMENT *Overview*

GUA	ELEMENT	COLOR	CHAKRA	MUSICAL NOTE	ESSENTIAL OILS	CRYSTALS
CAREER (N)	Water	Black Dark-tones	**Root** Heart	C F	Bergamot, *Clove*, Cypress, Ginger, Lemon, *Oregano*, Patchouli, Pine, Rosewood, Spruce, Vetiver	BLACK (element): Black Tourmaline, Black Obsidian, Black Onyx RED (chakra): Garnet, Red Amber, Red Coral, Red Jasper
KNOWLEDGE & SELF-CULTIVATION (NE)	*Earth*	Blues Greens	**Third Eye**	A	KNOWLEDGE: Lemon, *Peppermint*, Petitgrain, *Rosemary, Sage* SELF-CULTIVATION: Chamomile Roman, *Frankincense, Juniper*, Lemongrass, *Myrrh*	GREEN (element): Emerald, Green Flourite, Green Jade DARK BLUISH/ INDIGO (chakra): Azurite, Lapis lazuli, Sodalite
FAMILY & HEALTH (E)	Wood	Greens	**Heart** Root Sacral	F C D	Cypress, Geranium, Ginger, Pine, Sandalwood, Ylang ylang	GREEN (element): Aventurine, Emerald, Green Jade PINK (chakra): Pink Tourmaline, Rhodocrosite, Rhodonite, Rose Quartz
WEALTH & PROSPERITY (SE)	*Wood*	Purples Reds	**Solar Plexus** Crown Heart	E B F	Bergamot, *Cinnamon*, Cypress, Ginger, *Frankincense, Rosemary*, Spruce	PURPLE or RED (element): Amethyst, Cinnabar GOLDEN (chakra): Citrine, Gold, Tiger Eye
FAME & REPUTATION (S)	Fire	Reds	**Crown** Solar Plexus	B E	Bergamot, *Cedarwood*, *Frankincense, Myrrh*, Sandalwood	RED (element): Red Coral, Red Jade GOLDEN (chakra): Citrine, Gold

(continued on next page)

(continued from previous page)

FENG SHUI ENHANCEMENT *Overview*

GUA	ELEMENT	COLOR	CHAKRA	MUSICAL NOTE	ESSENTIAL OILS	CRYSTALS
RELATIONSHIPS, LOVE & MARRIAGE (SW)	*Earth*	Pinks Reds	**Heart** Sacral	F D	Jasmine, Lavender, Neroli, Orange, Pine, Rose, Sandalwood, Ylang ylang	PINK (element): Pink Tourmaline Rhodocrosite, Rhodonite, Rose Quartz GREEN (chakra): Aventurine, Malachite
CREATIVITY & CHILDREN (W)	Metal	White Pastels	**Sacral** Throat Heart	D G F	Bergamot, Chamomile Roman, Cypress, Geranium, Lavender, Mandarin, Orange, Pine, Rosewood, Sandalwood, Tangerine, Ylang ylang	WHITE / PASTEL / METAL (element): Amazonite, Aventurine, Gold, Pink Tourmaline, Smoky Quartz ORANGE (chakra): Carnelian, Citrine
HELPFUL PEOPLE & TRAVEL (NW)	*Metal*	Grays	**Throat** Third Eye	G A	Lavender, Lemon, ***Peppermint***, Pine, Rosewood	GRAY / METAL (element): Clear Quartz, Elestial Quartz BLUE (chakra): Aquamarine, Turquoise
TAI CHI: HEALTH & UNITY (CENTER)	Earth	Yellow Earth-tones	**Solar Plexus Heart**	E F	Eucalyptus, Globulus, Geranium, ***Juniper***, Lavender, Sandalwood, Spruce, Ylang ylang	GOLDEN (element & chakra): Amber, Citrine, Tiger Eye GREEN (chakra): Aventurine, Jade

Caution: Avoid essential oils in **bold italic** *during pregnancy.*

The direction indicated under the gua names apply when using the Compass Bagua Map. Otherwise, use the gua location according to the Non-directional Bagua Map on page 11.

Elements in italics are included in the Compass Bagua Map. Chakras in **bold** *are primary ones.*

"Real success is finding your lifework in the work that you love."

— David McCullough

5 Jump-Start Your Career

For many of us, our job, our vocation, our career play a big role in defining who we are as a person. Our feelings of self-worth are largely shaped and defined by the work we do. When this aspect of our life is fulfilling and rewarding, we feel good emotionally, mentally and physically. However, when our work environment is compromised in some way, it has a negative impact on our success in life.

Checklist For When You Want To Enhance Career

Do you want to:

- ☐ Increase your opportunities at work?
- ☐ Attract auspicious opportunities?
- ☐ Make a career change?

Do you feel that:

- ☐ Your career truly reflects whom you are inside?
- ☐ You enjoy and have a passion for your career?
- ☐ You have a fulfilling career that expresses your life's purpose?

If you would like to enhance your career—through a promotion, by starting your own business, or changing careers—take a look at the attributes and enhancements for this gua, and apply the natural holistic methods discussed in this chapter.

CAREER
Attributes & Enhancements

GUA ATTRIBUTES	ELEMENT	Water
	COLOR	Black, Darktones
	QUALITY	Courage
	CHAKRAS	Primary: Root Supporting: Heart
FENG SHUI ENHANCEMENTS	MUSICAL NOTES	Play music with the notes of C and F in this gua of your home.
	MATERIALS	Decorate with items that have black or dark tones. Water features, such as aquariums, fountains, ponds or pools. Objects with a reflective surface such as glass, mirror or cut crystal. Items that are asymmetrical, flowing, and free forming.
	ARTWORK	Paintings, photos and posters showing any of the above qualities or personal affirmations and inspirational quotes about Career.
LIFE GOALS ENHANCEMENTS	TLC PROCESS Affirmations, such as:	*"I enjoy and have passion for my career on all levels now."*
	ESSENTIAL OILS	Bergamot, ***Clove***, Cypress, Ginger, Lemon, ***Oregano***, Patchouli, Pine, Rosewood, Spruce, Vetiver
	CRYSTALS	Black stones (element): Black Obsidian, Black Onyx, Black Tourmaline Red stones (chakra): Garnet, Red Amber, Red Coral, Red Jasper Others: Amethyst, Azurite, Bloodstone, Citrine, Hematite, Jade, Malachite, Sodalite, Smoky Quartz, Tiger Eye

CAUTION: Avoid essential oils listed in **bold italic** during pregnancy.

About the Attributes

Career is located in the front center 1/3 of your home (or Compass Direction: N)—where security and confidence provide the foundation for success. Other issues related to career are courage and passion for your job and vocation/purpose. Do you have the courage to work in a career you like?

The element associated with this gua is Water. In Feng Shui, Water symbolizes wealth. The asymmetrical or flowing shapes of the Water element in this gua relate to Spirit and symbolize downward movement. Energetic qualities are deep, mysterious and insightful. It can connect us with inner truth and peace about our career and life.

BAGUA MAP

Wealth & Prosperity	Fame & Reputation	Relationships, Love & Marriage
Family & Health	Tai Chi: Health & Unity	Creativity & Children
Knowledge & Self-Cultivation	Career	Helpful People & Travel

ENTRANCE
or COMPASS DIRECTION: N

The primary chakra in the Career gua is the Root Chakra, located at the base of the spine, and associated with the color red. Consider: *Are you grounded, secureand confident that your career provides you the foundation for success?*

The supporting chakra is the Heart Chakra, located at the center of the chest and is associated with the color green. Consider: *Do you have the courage to pursue the career you desire? Are you passionate about what you do for a living?*

If you have any issues with this area of life, enhancing the Career area and implementing the Make It Happen Process™ may help improve your well-being and attract what you want.

Feng Shui for Career

You can use any of the following Feng Shui enhancements within your home to enhance Career:

- **Colors** that are black or dark tones. The black represents the depth of the water. Some will argue that blue should also represent water (Oriental Medicine).

- **Materials** that have water such as aquariums, fountains, ponds or pools. Just make sure that water is kept clean and flowing toward your home or office instead of out your door or window! Also any object that symbolizes water such as a reflective surface like glass, mirror and cut crystal. Any items that are asymmetrical, flowing, or free form in shape.

- **Artwork** including paintings, photos and posters depicting any of the above qualities or personal affirmations or inspirational quotes about Career.

TLC Process™ for Career

This method allows you to remove self-sabotage or "emotional blocks" using deprogramming or clearing statements, then reprogram with positive affirmations to better align yourself with your goals. Use the chart and workspace on the next page as a starting point for your own personal TLC Process™. For more information on the TLC Process™, see Chapter 4.

CAREER
TLC Process

	DEPROGRAMMING (Clearing)	REPROGRAMMING (Affirmation)
TLC PROCESS STATEMENT...	Tap on the side of your hand while saying your clearing statement 3 times: *"I deeply accept and love myself even though...*	Tap on top of your hand between the 4th and 5th knuckles while saying your affirmation statement *with feeling* 3 times: *"I totally and completely...*
	E X A M P L E S :	
...to Enhance LIFE GOALS	*...my career does not reflect whom I am inside."*	*...allow auspicious opportunities to come into my life on all levels now."*
	...I lack joy and passion for my career."	*...enjoy and have passion for my career on all levels now."*
	...I am afraid to make a career change."	*...look forward to making a career change on all levels now."*

Deprogramming Your Negative Belief(s):

"I deeply accept and love myself even though _____

_____ *."*

Reprogramming Your Positive Belief(s)/Affirmation(s):

"I totally and completely _____

_____ *on all levels now."*

Aromatherapy for Career

Use a blend of any of the following essential oils with the intention of finding the foundation, courage and confidence to enhance success in your Career. For more information on essential oils, see Chapter 4.

Bergamot: Facilitates strength, power, confidence and motivation. Relieves feelings of anxiety, stress and tension.

Clove: Promotes courage and protection.
Caution: Avoid during pregnancy.

Cypress: Produces a feeling of grounding and security. Facilitates confidence, strength and courage.

Ginger: Helps to provide direction and purpose by facilitating courage, confidence and strength.

Lemon: Enhances focus, clarity and concentration. Stimulates physical energy.

Oregano: Produces a sense of security.
Caution: Avoid during pregnancy.

Patchouli: Promotes relaxation, alleviates feelings of anxiety.

Pine: Facilitates forgiveness for self and others, acceptance of help, love and understanding. Reduces anxiety and rejuvenates the whole body.

Rosewood: Produces a sense of relaxation and peace.

Spruce: Grounding, producing the feeling of balance. Facilitates the release of emotional blocks.

Vetiver: Reduces stress by being emotionally calming, stabilizing and grounding.

Crystal Therapy for Career

Select a crystal that resonates with you. Then personalize it with your affirmation. Place the crystal over your written affirmation somewhere in this gua. For more information on crystals, see Chapter 4.

Use BLACK crystals to represent the color associated with Career

Black Tourmaline: Acts as a protective shield against negativity from self and others.

Black Obsidian: Promotes grounding and emotional security. Protects emotional draining from others. Sharpens visions and helps with transitions.

Black Onyx: Assists in making wise decisions. Encourages good fortune and happiness.

Use REDDISH crystals to enhance the Root Chakra, which supports Career

Garnet: Known as a "stone of commitment" to oneself, others and purpose.

Red Amber: Provides grounding and protection.

Red Coral: Stimulates the energetic pursuit of goals. May also protect against depression.

Red Jasper: Promotes grounding and helps to reduce fears and insecurities.

Other color crystals that also can enhance Career

Amethyst: Enhances strength and stability.

Azurite: Aids in finding direction.

Bloodstone: Enhances abilities, talents and decision-making processes.

Citrine: Provides a sense of stability and emotional balance. Facilitates a rational approach toward challenges.

Hematite: Provides a state of mind that allows grounding, harmony and emotional clarity.

Jade: Known as a "dream stone," it helps one to realize their devotion to one's purpose. Facilitates confidence, self-sufficiency, self-reliance and self-assuredness.

Malachite: Assists in achieving desired goal.

Sodalite: Helps to provide direction of purpose with light-heartedness.

Smoky Quartz: Good for grounding. Known as a "stone of cooperation," it enhances unification of thoughts directed toward the same goal.

Tiger Eye: Facilitates self-confidence, inner strength and stability to be more grounded.

Aspiring Actress

Stephanie, an aspiring actress of 20, was lacking opportunities for auditions. They came sporadically. One month, she would be called for two or three auditions, while the next month there would be none.

Implementing the Make It Happen Process™

1) *Stephanie used the TLC Process™ for clearing the way to attract opportunities for a successful acting career.*

   - *STEP A Deprogramming:*
     While tapping on the side of her hand, (see page 50), she repeated the following statement 3 times:

     "I deeply accept, love and honor myself even though I lack opportunities for a successful acting career on all levels now."

   - *STEP B Reprogramming with positive affirmation:*
     While tapping on the top of her hand (see page 51), she repeated the following statement 3 times:

     "I am in the right place at the right time to attract opportunities for a successful acting career on all levels now."

2) *Stephanie set her intentions by applying a blend of essential oils (see page 72) to the Career (and Helpful People) areas of her home with a room spray to enhance the opportunities for more auditions and parts in films.*

The Results

The results were immediate! Stephanie had gone about two months without a single audition and the day after she started using the aromatherapy, her agent called with a national commercial audition. From that point on, the auditions have been averaging two or three a week, including one for a major athletic shoe and apparel brand. She was also contacted by a talent manager who is interested in representing her, and she was cast in a short film. A dream come true for an aspiring actress!

Hard Worker

Suzie was a 58-year-old woman who had been working as an instructor at a school in the San Diego area for seven years. She found herself unhappy with her job, working many more hours than she wanted. Suzie had not received a raise in that time and felt unappreciated. During her Feng Shui consultation, it was interesting to note that her Career area of the home was missing as well. Her goal was to get paid more for all her hard work and overtime and feel more appreciated for all her work at the school.

Implementing the Make It Happen Process™

1) Suzie used the TLC Process™ for clearing the way to remove the self-sabotage of not deserving better pay and replacing it with a new empowering affirmation.

- *STEP A Deprogramming: While tapping on the side of her hand, (see page 50), she repeated the following statement 3 times:*

   "I deeply accept, love and honor myself even though I lack reward for my work and make less money than I desire on all levels now."

- *STEP B Reprogramming with positive affirmation: While tapping on the top of her hand (see page 51), she repeated the following statement 3 times:*

   "I am rewarded for my work and allow myself to make more money on all levels now."

2) She set her intentions by applying a blend of essential oils (see page 72) to her Root Chakra, grounding the career she wanted, and to the Heart Chakra to support her passion for her job.

3) Suzie also personalized and placed a big black tourmaline (see page 72) over her written affirmation in the Career area of her home.

The Results

Within two weeks of doing this process, Suzie received a $10,000 raise! It was time for evaluations and her upper management was very appreciative of all her good work over the past few years and felt that Suzie was in need of a very well deserved raise. Suzie is much happier now that she is getting paid more and also feels more appreciated for her work.

Several months later, she had another review and was given another raise. Her evaluation reflected "exceed expectations" in all areas. Suzie is still amazed to this day.

"Science is organized knowledge.
Wisdom is organized life."

— Immanuel Kant

6 Increase Your Knowledge & Self-Cultivation

Reaching our full capacity intellectually, emotionally and spiritually gives us a sense of awakening and enlightenment. In our quest for self-cultivation, we seek knowledge and a sense of purpose. Left unfulfilled in this regard, we feel an emptiness or lack of peace.

Checklist For When You Want To Enhance Knowledge & Self-Cultivation

Do you want to:

☐ Increase your knowledge in a certain area of expertise?

☐ Do well in school?

☐ Cultivate your own spiritual growth, balance and harmony?

Do you feel that:

☐ You are doing something in your life to promote and enhance your personal spiritual growth?

☐ You enjoy and allow time of quietness just for yourself? This can include meditation, study or reading time.

☐ You have a balance of study (knowledge and professional growth) and quiet time in your life?

If you would like to increase your knowledge and self-cultivation, review the attributes and enhancements of this gua shown below, and apply the natural holistic methods discussed in this chapter.

KNOWLEDGE & SELF-CULTIVATION
Attributes & Enhancements

GUA ATTRIBUTES	ELEMENT	Earth (Mountain)
	COLOR	Blues & Greens
	QUALITY	Stillness
	CHAKRAS	Third Eye
FENG SHUI ENHANCEMENTS	MUSICAL NOTES	Play music that has the musical notes of A in this gua of your home.
	MATERIALS	Decorate with items that are blue and green that have knowledge or materials you are currently studying such as books, tapes and DVDs.
	ARTWORK	Statue of a meditative figure such as Buddha. Paintings, pictures and posters showing mountains, gardens, or a meditative figure. Also, personal affirmations and inspirational quotes associated with this gua.
LIFE GOALS ENHANCEMENTS	TLC PROCESS Affirmations, such as:	*"I have a healthy balance of studying and stillness in my life on all levels now."*
	ESSENTIAL OILS	Knowledge: Eucalyptus, Lemon, ***Peppermint***, Petitgrain, ***Rosemary, Sage*** Self-Cultivation: Chamomile Roman, ***Frankincense***, ***Juniper***, Lemongrass, ***Myrrh***
	CRYSTALS	Green stones (element): Emerald, Green Flourite, Green Jade Dark-Bluish/Indigo stones (chakra): Azurite, Lapis lazuli, Sodalite Others: Amethyst, Aquamarine, Blue-Lace Agate, Celestite, Hematite, Clear & Smoky Quartz, Turquoise

CAUTION: Avoid essential oils listed in ***bold italic*** during pregnancy.

About the Attributes

Knowledge & Self-Cultivation is located in the front left 1/3 corner of your home (or Compass Direction: NE)—where the environment for learning and spiritual growth can thrive. Stillness is a quality associated with this gua and is important for learning knowledge, meditation and contemplating about life and one's spiritual growth. Other qualities associated with this area include intuition, wisdom, inner vision, awakening and self-cultivation.

The element related to Knowledge & Self-Cultivation is Earth. The earth energy in this gua is that of the mountain, where you can go and experience stillness for contemplation and meditation.

The chakra associated with this gua is the Third Eye Chakra located at the center of the forehead just above and between the eyebrows. It is associated with the color indigo. Consider: *Are you connected with your intuitive center (third-eye) to access knowledge, wisdom and gain spiritual growth?*

If you have any issues with this area of life, enhancing the Knowledge & Self-Cultivation area and implementing the Make It Happen Process™ may help improve your well-being and attract what you want.

BAGUA MAP

Wealth & Prosperity	Fame & Reputation	Relationships, Love & Marriage
Family & Health	Tai Chi: Health & Unity	Creativity & Children
Knowledge & Self-Cultivation	Career	Helpful People & Travel

ENTRANCE
or COMPASS DIRECTION: NE

Feng Shui for Knowledge & Self-Cultivation

You can decorate with or use any of the following representations to enhance Knowledge & Self-Cultivation:

- Colors that have blues and greens.

- Materials that have knowledge or you are currently studying such as books, tapes and DVDs.

- Artwork such as a statue of a meditative figure such as Buddha, paintings, pictures and posters showing mountains, gardens, or Buddha. Also, personal affirmations and inspirational quotes associated with Knowledge & Self-Cultivation.

TLC Process™ for Knowledge & Self-Cultivation

This method allows you to remove self-sabotage or "emotional blocks" using deprogramming or clearing statements, then reprogram with positive affirmations to better align yourself with your goals. Use the chart and workspace as a starting point for your own personal TLC Process™. For more information on the TLC Process™, see Chapter 4.

KNOWLEDGE & SELF-CULTIVATION
TLC Process

	DEPROGRAMMING (Clearing)	REPROGRAMMING (Affirmation)
TLC PROCESS STATEMENT...	Tap on the side of your hand while saying your clearing statement 3 times: *"I deeply accept and love myself even though...*	Tap on top of your hand between the 4th and 5th knuckles while saying your affirmation statement *with feeling* 3 times: *"I totally and completely...*
	EXAMPLES:	
...to Enhance LIFE GOALS	*...I lack motivation to promote my spiritual growth."*	*...am motivated and actively promoting and enhancing personal spiritual growth on all levels now."*
	...I lack quiet time for myself."	*...enjoy and allow quiet time just for myself on all levels now."*
	...I lack a healthy balance of studying and stillness in my life."	*...have a healthy balance of studying and stillness in my life on all levels now."*

Deprogramming Your Negative Belief(s):

"I deeply accept and love myself even though _____
_____ *."*

Reprogramming Your Positive Belief(s) / Affirmation(s):

"I totally and completely _____
_____ *on all levels now."*

Aromatherapy for Knowledge & Self-Cultivation

Use a blend of any of the following oils with the intention of creating mental clarity, wisdom and pursuit of self-cultivation. For more information on essential oils, see Chapter 4.

KNOWLEDGE:

Eucalyptus globulus: Facilitates concentration, logical thought and positive change.

Jasmine: May enhance wisdom and intuition.

Lemon: Enhances focus, clarity and concentration.

Peppermint, Sage: Stimulates and promotes concentration. Helps to reduce mental fatigue.
Caution: Avoid during pregnancy with both essential oils.

Petitgrain: Uplifting. Enhances memory. Eases mental fatigue and helps to clear confusion.

Rosemary: Enhances memory.
Caution: Avoid during pregnancy.

SELF-CULTIVATION:

Chamomile, Roman: Facilitates peace, joy and relaxation. Balances emotions.

Frankincense: Promotes meditation and spiritual awareness. Facilitates wisdom and inspiration.
Caution: Avoid during pregnancy.

Juniper: May promote one's spiritual awareness.
Caution: Avoid during pregnancy.

Lemongrass: Enhances psychic awareness.

Myrrh: Facilitates spiritual awareness.
Caution: Avoid during pregnancy.

Crystal Therapy for Knowledge & Self-Cultivation

Choose a crystal that resonates with you then personalize it with your affirmation. Place the crystal over your written affirmation somewhere in this gua. For more information on crystals, see Chapter 4.

Use GREEN to represent the color associated with Knowledge & Self-Cultivation

Emerald: Enhances memory, intelligence and wisdom.

Green Flourite: Enhances understanding, mental concentration and capacity.

Green Jade: Enhances courage, clarity and tranquility of the mind.

Use INDIGO/DARK BLUE-ISH crystals to enhance the Third Eye Chakra, which supports Knowledge & Self-Cultivation

Azurite: Assists in meditation. Calms the mind to assist in reaching the state of "no mind."

Lapis Lazuli: Enhances mental endurance, wisdom to understand information, insight and good judgment.

Sodalite: Helps clear and balance the third eye. Assists in rational mental processes and logical thinking.

Other crystals that can enhance Knowledge & Self-Cultivation

Amethyst: As a stone for meditation, it enhances relaxation, meditation and spiritual insight.

Aquamarine: Facilitates calmness, peace and meditation. Assists in attuning one to higher spiritual awareness.

Blue-Lace Agate: Assists in reaching higher states of awareness and spiritual realms.

Celestite: Assists in mental activities.

Clear Quartz: Enhances mental clarity, meditation and spiritual development.

Hematite: Provides a calming atmosphere, while at the same time enhancing memory and mental attunement. Helps to sort out thoughts in the mind.

Smoky Quartz: Enhances mental clarity and meditation.

Turquoise: Facilitates mental relaxation, stress reduction and attunement.

To Retain or Not to Retain

Patti, a 58-year-old woman, was looking for a career change. She decided to become a real estate agent and enrolled in an online licensing course. Patti led a busy life and her rusty skills made studying a real chore. In fact, she avoided it as much as possible. Not only did Patti have a difficult time studying, it was also a challenge for her to retain information and focus on the subject matter.

Implementing the Make It Happen Process™

1) *Patti used the TLC Process™ for clearing the way to deprogram her inability to study and retain knowledge and reprogram with her empowering positive affirmation.*

   - *STEP A Deprogramming:*
     While tapping on the side of her hand, (see page 50), Patti repeated the following statement 3 times:

     "I deeply accept, love and honor myself even though I lack motivation to study and forget information I have learned on all levels now."

   - *STEP B Reprogramming with positive affirmation:*
     While tapping on the top of her hand (see page 51), Patti repeated the following statement 3 times:

     "I am totally and completely motivated and look forward to studying and retaining all knowledge I have learned on all levels now."

2) *Patti set her intentions by applying a blend of essential oils (see page 72) to the Knowledge & Self-Cultivation area of her home with a room spray and a body oil to her Third Eye Chakra to enhance concentration and retention of knowledge from the course.*

3) *She also personalized and placed a green jade Buddha (see page 72) over her written affirmation in the Knowledge & Self-Cultivation area of her home.*

   (continued on next page)

(continued from previous page)

The Results

After utilizing the TLC methods for a few days, Patti was able to comprehend and retain more of the study material with greater ease. Incorporating the Feng Shui aromatherapy and a personalized jade Buddha figurine into the process seemed to intensify the benefits of the TLC Process™ for Patti. She was able to complete chapters in a quarter of the time it took before. Patti now looks forward to finishing her real estate course with the perfect test scores she has been achieving. She plans on using these same methods to enhance other areas in her life.

Wandering Mind

Joe wanted to meditate. However, he found it difficult to focus and concentrate on "nothing." His mind kept wandering off thinking about all the things he still needed to do. As a result, Joe found it difficult to set aside time to meditate.

Joe set his intentions by applying a blend of essential oils (see page 72) to the Knowledge & Self-Cultivation area of his home with a room spray and a body oil to his Third Eye Chakra to enhance concentration for meditation. Soon, he found that it was much easier to meditate and as a bonus also found more time to work on his own spiritual growth.

"Your family and your love
must be cultivated like a garden.
Time, effort, and imagination
must be summoned constantly
to keep it flourishing and growing."

— Jim Rohn

7 Cultivate Your Family & Health

Family and Health are at the core of our existence. Keeping these aspects of our life in harmony is critical to our physical and emotional stability. Do you enjoy the best of your family and health?

Checklist For When You Want To Enhance Family & Health

Do you want to:

- ☐ Enhance your health?
- ☐ Recover from an illness?
- ☐ Improve your family relations?

Do you feel that:

- ☐ Your family life is good, creating harmony within your home and your body?
- ☐ You resolve family issues, and therefore are at peace, which reduces stress and enhances your health?
- ☐ You have heart-to-heart talks with family members, including your children?
- ☐ You have and enjoy loving harmonious relationships with family and relatives?
- ☐ You have excellent health on all levels?

If you would like to cultivate harmony in your family and health, review the attributes and enhancements of this gua shown below, and apply the natural holistic methods discussed in this chapter.

FAMILY & HEALTH
Attributes & Enhancements

GUA ATTRIBUTES	ELEMENT	Wood
	COLOR	Green
	QUALITY	Strength
	CHAKRAS	Primary: Heart Supporting: Root, Sacral
FENG SHUI ENHANCEMENTS	MUSICAL NOTES	Play music with the notes of F, C and D in this gua of your home.
	MATERIALS	Decorate with items that have green; objects that look like columns such as tree trunks, poles, columns, and stripes. Items made of wood such as plants, flowers, furniture, decks and paneling. Cloths and textiles made from fabric such as cotton and hemp.
	ARTWORK	Photos of family members. Paintings and posters depicting any of the above qualities, such as landscapes, flowers, trees, gardens, etc. Personal affirmations or inspirational sayings about Family & Health.
LIFE GOALS ENHANCEMENTS	TLC PROCESS Affirmation, such as:	*"I attract and have loving and harmonious relationships with family members on all levels now."*
	ESSENTIAL OILS	Cypress, Geranium, Ginger, Pine, Sandalwood, Ylang ylang
	CRYSTALS	Green stones (element & chakra): Aventurine, Emerald, Green Jade Pink stones (chakra): Pink Tourmaline, Rhodocrosite, Rhodonite, Rose Quartz Others: Citrine, Garnet, Gold, Lapis lazuli

About the Attributes

Family & Health is located in the middle left 1/3 of your home (or Compass Direction: E) where strength can assist in staying emotionally and physically balanced. Good health and family relationships can provide a strong foundation for growth and happiness.

BAGUA MAP

Wealth & Prosperity	Fame & Reputation	Relationships, Love & Marriage
Family & Health	Tai Chi: Health & Unity	Creativity & Children
Knowledge & Self-Cultivation	Career	Helpful People & Travel

ENTRANCE
or COMPASS DIRECTION: E

The element related to the Family & Health area is Wood. The column shape of the Wood element symbolizes upward movement and growth, and represents pioneering and progressive thought. Its energetic qualities are flexible, active and fast-paced. The wood element in Family & Health has to do with continued new growth between family members.

The primary chakra of this gua is the Heart Chakra, located over your heart center and is associated with the color green. It is interesting to note that the color green is also associated with this gua. Consider: *Do you have love and forgiveness for your family members?*

There are two supporting chakras in Family & Health—the Root and Sacral Chakras. The Root Chakra is located at the base of the spine and associated with the color red. Consider: Do you have a strong foundation and sense of tribal unity with your family? The Sacral Chakra is located between the base of the spine and the navel and is associated with the color orange. This chakra is associated with health, family and the need for relationships. Consider: *Are you able to access your feelings and emotions to deal with family issues?*

If you have any issues with this area of life, enhancing the Family & Health area and implementing the Make It Happen Process™ may help improve your well-being and attract what you want.

Feng Shui for Family & Health

You can decorate with or use any of the following representations to enhance Family & Health:

- **Colors** that are green.

- **Shapes** of objects that look like columns such as tree trunks, poles, columns and stripes.

- **Materials** that are made of wood, such as plants, flowers, furniture, decks and paneling. Cloths and textiles, such as cotton or hemp.

- **Artwork** including paintings and posters showing or incorporating any of the above qualities. Artwork that shows landscaping, flowers, trees, gardens, etc. Photos of family members. Personal affirmations or inspirational quotes associated with Family & Health.

TLC Process™ for Family & Health

This natural method allows you to remove self-sabotage or "emotional blocks" using deprogramming or clearing statements, then reprogram with positive affirmations to better align yourself with your goals. See examples in chart on the next page. For more information on the TLC Process™, see Chapter 4.

FAMILY & HEALTH
TLC Process

	DEPROGRAMMING (Clearing)	REPROGRAMMING (Affirmation)
TLC PROCESS STATEMENT...	Tap on the side of your hand while saying your clearing statement 3 times: **"I deeply accept and love myself even though...**	Tap on top of your hand between the 4th and 5th knuckles while saying your affirmation statement *with feeling* 3 times: **"I totally and completely...**
	EXAMPLES:	
...to Enhance LIFE GOALS	...I lack loving harmonious relationships with family members and relatives."	...attract and have loving harmonious relationships with family members and relatives on all levels now."
	...I have unresolved family issues which increases stress and a state of dis-ease."	...release all negative feelings and resolve all family issues which reduces stress and puts me at ease for optimum health on all levels now."
	...my health is compromised."	...have excellent health on all levels now."

Deprogramming Your Negative Belief(s):

"I deeply accept and love myself even though _____
_____ ."

Reprogramming Your Positive Belief(s)/Affirmation(s):

"I totally and completely _____
_____ *on all levels now."*

Aromatherapy for Family & Health

Use a blend of any of the following essential oils with the intention of allowing love, compassion and peace to come in harmony with family members, as well as enhance health. For more information on essential oils, see Chapter 4.

Cypress: Produces a feeling of grounding and security.
Facilitates confidence, strength and courage.

Geranium: Facilitates creativity, security and balance.
Promotes feelings of well-being and peace.
Uplifting and assists in balancing the emotions.

Ginger: Promotes courage, confidence and strength.

Pine: Facilitates forgiveness for self and others, acceptance of
help, love and understanding. Reduces anxiety and rejuvenates
the whole body.

Sandalwood: Facilitates self-awareness, balance and connection.
Facilitates joy, self-esteem, and self-image. Facilitates balance,
unity and healing. Helps to neutralize manipulation, obsession
and aggression. Assists in calming and balancing the emotions.

Ylang ylang: Promotes feelings of peace, joy, self-love and confidence.
Promotes unification. Reduces resentment, jealousy and frustration.

Crystal Therapy for Family & Health

Select a crystal that resonates with you and personalize it with your affirmation. Place the crystal over your written affirmation somewhere in this gua. For more information on crystals, see Chapter 4.

Use GREEN crystals to represent the color associated with this gua and to enhance the Heart Chakra which supports Family & Health

Aventurine: Aids in emotional stabilization.

Emerald: Strengthens memory, foresight and wisdom. Enhances speech and creativity.

Green Jade: Promotes understanding and cohesiveness of groups. Helps to provide the ability to bring together and improve dysfunctional relationships.

Use PINK crystals to heal the heart emotionally and enhance the Heart Chakra which supports Family & Health

Pink Tourmaline: Receiving love and giving love joyfully.

Rhodocrosite: Known as a "stone of love and balance," it enhances love for self and others. Eases emotional pains.

Rhodonite: Known as a "stone of love," it resonates to unconditional love. Enhances self-worth, self-confidence and self-esteem.

Rose Quartz: As a "stone of gentle love," it enhances feelings and abilities to give and receive love and compassion, including self-love.

Other color crystals that also can enhance Family & Health

Citrine: Helps to smooth over group and family problems, thus producing cohesiveness within that group.

Garnet: Known as a "stone of health."

Gold: Attracts cooperation and receptivity.

Lapis lazuli: Helps relationships to be successful.

Overwhelmed Mother

Lisa, a 35-year wife and mother, had disharmonious family relations. Her husband did not help around the house and her children, two and five years old, were a challenge to manage.

Implementing the Make It Happen Process™

1) Lisa did the TLC Process™ for clearing the way to create more harmony among family members:

- *STEP A Deprogramming:*
  While tapping on the side of her hand, (see page 50), she repeated the following statement 3 times:

  "I deeply accept, love and honor myself even though I lack harmony with my family members on all levels now."

- *STEP B Reprogramming with positive affirmation:*
  While tapping on the top of her hand (see page 51), she repeated the following statement 3 times:

  "I am surrounded by my family with harmony on all levels now."

2) Lisa set her intentions by applying a blend of essential oils (see page 72) to the Family & Health area of her home with a room spray and a body oil to her Heart chakra which supports the Family & Health area.

3) Lisa then personalized and placed a large tumbled aventurine crystal (see page 72) on top of her written affirmation in the Family & Health area of her home.

The Results

Within a week of implementing the Make It Happen Process™, Lisa's husband started helping around the house. She found herself less stressed and able to manage her children and their activities much easier. Lisa also noticed a better sense of well-being.

Great Grandparenting

Tom and Jodi had family members that lived nearby. Jodi found herself babysitting her grandchildren about four hours a day, at least three times during the week. In addition, Tom and Jodi found themselves watching the kids on weekends as well! Although they loved their grandchildren, they both felt that they were being taken advantage of. Tom and Jodi wanted to be able to talk to their daughter-in-law about the situation with love and harmony. However, things were usually taken personally.

Implementing the Make It Happen Process™

1) Tom and Jodi implemented the TLC Process™ *for clearing the way to communicate honestly and lovingly with family members.*

- *STEP A Deprogramming:*
  While tapping on the side of their hands, (see page 50), Tom and Jodi repeated the following statement 3 times:

  "I deeply accept, love and honor myself even though I lack harmony with my family members on all levels now."

- *STEP B Reprogramming with positive affirmation:*
  While tapping on the top of their hands (see page 51), Tom and Jodi repeated the following statement 3 times:

  "We are able to talk to our family members with honesty, love and harmony on all levels now."

2) The couple set their intentions by applying a blend of essential oils (see page 72) to the Family & Health area of their home with a room spray and a body oil blend for the Heart Chakra which supports the Family & Health area.

3) Then they personalized and placed an aventurine stone (see page 72) on top of their written affirmation in the Family & Health area of their home.

The Results

After about a week of using the Make It Happen Process™ *and talking to their daughter-in-law, Tom and Jodi came to an understanding with her about how often they were asked to babysit the grandchildren. Interestingly enough, everyone was able to communicate without stress or emotional charge. Now, the couple only babysits their grandchildren about two times a month. They enjoy watching the children without resentment or feeling they are being taken advantage of.*

"The more you express gratitude
for what you have, the more you
will have to express gratitude for."

— Zig Ziglar

8 Welcome Wealth & Prosperity

Having prosperity in all aspects of life can bring us great joy and peace. When we have an abundance of good health, positive relationships and a steady income, we feel good emotionally and physically. Would you like more prosperity in *your* life?

Checklist For When You Want To Enhance Wealth & Prosperity

Do you want to:

☐ Increase cash flow?

☐ Have prosperity in other aspects of your life, such as good health, career opportunities, and good relationship with your significant other?

Do you feel that:

☐ Wealth and prosperity continuously manifests and flows into your life easily?

☐ You welcome and accept continuous abundance in all aspects of your life?

☐ You have an abundance of all you need?

If you would like to welcome more wealth and prosperity into your life, review the attributes and enhancements of this gua shown below, and apply the natural holistic methods discussed in this chapter.

WEALTH & PROSPERITY
Attributes & Enhancements

GUA ATTRIBUTES	ELEMENT	Wood
	COLOR	Purples & Reds
	QUALITY	Gratitude
	CHAKRAS	Primary: Solar Plexus Supporting: Crown, Heart
FENG SHUI ENHANCEMENTS	MUSICAL NOTES	Play music with the notes of E, B and F in this gua of your home.
	MATERIALS	Decorate with items that have purples and reds; plants with rounded leaves, such as a ficus tree or jade plant, and plants that represent growth such as fortune bamboo and money tree; items and materials that look elegant and feel rich.
	ARTWORK	Paintings, pictures and posters of images that represent abundance to you, such as money, cars and jewelry. Also, personal affirmations and inspirational quotes associated with Wealth and Prosperity.
LIFE GOALS ENHANCEMENTS	TLC PROCESS Affirmation, such as:	*"I manifest a steady flow of wealth and prosperity into my life on all levels now."*
	ESSENTIAL OILS	Bergamot, ***Cinnamon***, Cypress, Ginger, ***Frankincense***, ***Rosemary***, Spruce
	CRYSTALS	Purple & Red stones (element): Amethyst, Cinnabar Yellow/Golden stones (chakra): Citrine, Gold, Tiger Eye Others: Turquoise, Diamond, Ruby

CAUTION: Avoid essential oils listed in ***bold italic*** during pregnancy.

About the Attributes

Wealth & Prosperity is located in the back left 1/3 corner of your home (or Compass Direction: SE)—where personal power and gratitude can enhance prosperity. Wealth & Prosperity goes beyond money. It also includes abundance in all aspects of your life, including health and happiness.

Here in this area, the Wood element relates to the potential of continued growth and expansion of one's wealth and prosperity in all areas of life. The column shape of the Wood element symbolizes upward movement and growth. Its energetic qualities are flexible, active and fast-paced. It represents pioneering and progressive thought.

BAGUA MAP

Wealth & Prosperity	Fame & Reputation	Relationships, Love & Marriage
Family & Health	Tai Chi: Health & Unity	Creativity & Children
Knowledge & Self-Cultivation	Career	Helpful People & Travel

ENTRANCE
or COMPASS DIRECTION: SE

This gua is associated with the color purple. Historically, the color purple has been worn by royalty and is often associated with wealth and prosperity. Water fountains can also be used in this area to welcome prosperity. In Feng Shui, water symbolizes wealth. The Water element also helps "nourish" the Wood element associated with this gua.

The primary chakra in the Wealth & Prosperity gua is the Solar Plexus, located between the navel and bottom of the breastbone. It is associated with the color yellow. This is where you get that "gut feeling." Consider: *Do you have the personal power to attract wealth and prosperity in your life?*

This gua also has two supporting chakras: Crown and Heart. The Crown Chakra is located on the top of your head and is associated with the color violet. Consider: *Do you attract wealth and prosperity at the higher spiritual levels?*

The Heart Chakra is located over the center of your chest and is associated with the color green. Consider: *Do you have gratitude for what you do have in your life?* Having gratitude for what you do have allows you to attract more abundance. Your energy goes in the direction of what you are focusing on. Therefore, focus on what you do have rather than what you lack.

If you have any issues with this area of life, enhancing the Wealth & Prosperity area and implementing the Make It Happen Process™ may help improve your well-being and attract what you want.

Feng Shui for Wealth & Prosperity

You can decorate with or use any combination of the following to enhance Wealth & Prosperity:

- **Colors** that are purples and reds.

- **Plants** such as the ficus tree or jade plant that have rounded leaves, which symbolize an abundance of coins. Also, plants that represent growth, such as fortune bamboo and the money tree.

- **Materials** that look rich, such as fine cut crystals, or materials which are elegant and feel rich.

- **Artwork** such as paintings, pictures and posters of images that represent abundance to you, such as money, cars, jewelry, personal affirmations or inspirational quotes associated with Wealth & Prosperity.

TLC Process™ for Wealth & Prosperity

This method allows you to remove self-sabotage or "emotional blocks" using deprogramming or clearing statements, then reprogram with positive affirmations to better align yourself with your goals. Use the chart and workspace on the next page as idea starters for your personalized TLC Process™. For more details on this method, see Chapter 4.

WEALTH & PROSPERITY
TLC Process

	DEPROGRAMMING (Clearing)	REPROGRAMMING (Affirmation)
TLC PROCESS STATEMENT...	Tap on the side of your hand while saying your clearing statement 3 times: *"I deeply accept and love myself even though...*	Tap on top of your hand between the 4th and 5th knuckles while saying your affirmation statement *with feeling* 3 times: *"I totally and completely...*
	E X A M P L E S :	
...to Enhance LIFE GOALS	*...I lack a steady flow of wealth and prosperity in my life."*	*...manifest a steady flow of wealth and prosperity into my life on all levels now."*
	...I lack a continuous abundance in all aspects of my life."	*...welcome and accept continuous abundance in all aspects of my life, including wealth, health and happiness on all levels now."*
	...I lack an abundance of all that I need."	*...have an abundance of all that I need on all levels now."*

Deprogramming Your Negative Belief(s):

"I deeply accept and love myself even though _____
_____."

Reprogramming Your Positive Belief(s)/Affirmation(s):

"I totally and completely _____
_____ *on all levels now."*

Aromatherapy for Wealth & Prosperity

Use a blend of any of the following essential oils with the intention of attracting an abundance of wealth, health and happiness; and having gratitude for what you have. For more information on essential oils, see Chapter 4.

Bergamot: Facilitates confidence, strength, power and motivation.

Cinnamon: Believed to have a frequency that attracts wealth.
Caution: Avoid during pregnancy.

Cypress: Produces a feeling of grounding and security. Facilitates confidence, strength and courage.

Ginger: Helps to provide direction and purpose by facilitating courage, confidence and strength. May influence money.

Frankincense: Facilitates wisdom, inspiration, performance and emotional stability.
Caution: Avoid during pregnancy.

Rosemary: Believed to attract wealth.
Caution: Avoid during pregnancy.

Spruce: Believed to attract wealth.

Crystal Therapy for Wealth & Prosperity

Select a crystal that resonates with you and personalize it with your affirmation. Place the crystal over your written affirmation somewhere in this gua. For more information on crystals, see Chapter 4.

Use these PURPLE or RED crystals to represent the color associated with Wealth & Prosperity

Amethyst: May help business affairs prosper. May attract an abundance of prosperity in other aspects of your life as well by focusing love and gratitude into the amethyst.

Cinnabar: Also known as a "merchant's stone," it assists in accumulating and maintaining wealth.

Ruby: Promotes stability of wealth.

Use YELLOW and GOLDEN crystals to enhance the Solar Plexus Chakra, which supports Wealth & Prosperity

Citrine: Known as a "merchant's stone," it is thought to assist in accumulating and maintaining a state of wealth.

Gold: Attracts wealth.

Tiger Eye: Attracts and maintains wealth.

Other color crystals that a can enhance Wealth & Prosperity

Diamond: Enhances the manifestation of abundance in all areas of life.

Green Tourmaline: Attracts abundance and prosperity.

Malachite: Enhances good fortune and success in business.

Turquoise: Attracts prosperity and abundance.

Hit and Miss

Brandon owned his own business. He found that jobs came in spurts. Brandon wanted to attract a steady flow of work and more reliable income.

Implementing the Make It Happen Process™

1) Brandon used the TLC Process™ for clearing the way to attract a steady flow of income.

- *STEP A Deprogramming:*
  While tapping on the side of his hand (see page 50), he repeated the following statement 3 times:

  "I deeply accept, love and honor myself even though I block an abundant flow of financial wealth on all levels now."

- *STEP B Reprogramming with positive affirmation:*
  While tapping on the top of his hand (see page 51), he repeated the following statement 3 times:

  "I am abundant, open and attract a steady flow of income; financial wealth comes to me easily on all levels now."

2) He set his intentions by applying a blend of essential oils (see page 72) to the Wealth & Prosperity area of his home and a body oil blend for the Solar Plexus and Crown chakras that supported the Wealth & Prosperity area.

3) Brandon then personalized and placed citrine and tiger eye tumbled stones (see page 72) on top of his written affirmation in the Wealth & Prosperity area of his home.

The Results

Brandon experienced a major shift in his workload within the first week of starting the Make It Happen Process™. In fact, Brandon found himself so busy he had to turn down work! For the first time ever, Brandon's income doubled, and he continues to attract and receive a steady flow of income.

Dream Home

Beatrex contacted me after reading an article I had written for a local magazine for the Western School of Feng Shui™ on essential oils associated with the different areas of the bagua map.

Beatrex was very impressed and began using essential oils (see page 72) for the Wealth & Prosperity gua. She used the blends everyday rubbing them on her Solar Plexus Chakra while saying her affirmation.

Beatrex experienced amazing results. She manifested her dream home on the beach, something that had been on her manifest list for many years...a dream come true.

Her friends also used the aromatherapy blend. One friend embarked an all-expenses-paid trip on a luxury liner cruise ship. Another friend used it on her show dogs and they won the grand championships all year. Then, they were asked to appear on the cover of a major pet store magazine and became very profitable models in the pet world.

"A good reputation is more
valuable than money."

— Publius Syrus

9 Boost Your Fame & Reputation

As children, we gain great satisfaction in being recognized for our talents, accomplishments and good deeds, no matter how small. As adults, we continue to yearn for appreciation, recognition and respect at work, at home and in the community. Have you achieved your personal best?

Checklist For When You Want To Enhance Fame & Reputation

Do you want to:

☐ Have more recognition at work?
☐ Be well known for something you do?
☐ Establish a good relationship in your community?

Do you feel that:

☐ You project to the world the person you truly are?
☐ You are appreciated, respected, and recognized for your skills, knowledge and accomplishments?
☐ Your good reputation is well known with your colleagues and throughout your community?

If you would like to receive appreciation and recognition, review the attributes and enhancements of this gua shown below, and apply the natural holistic methods discussed in this chapter.

FAME & REPUTATION
Attributes & Enhancements

GUA ATTRIBUTES	ELEMENT	Fire
	COLOR	Red
	QUALITY	Integrity
	CHAKRAS	Primary: Crown Supporting: Solar Plexus
FENG SHUI ENHANCEMENTS	MUSICAL NOTES	Play music with the notes of B and E in this gua of your home.
	MATERIALS	Decorate with items that are red, shaped like a triangle, cone or pyramid; items that have or generate lighting; animal-based materials, such as feathers, wool, and leather.
	ARTWORK	Paintings, pictures and certificates that represent your accomplishments, such as awards, diplomas, trophies or personal affirmations and inspirational quotes associated with Fame & Reputation.
LIFE GOALS ENHANCEMENTS	TLC PROCESS Affirmations, such as:	*"I am appreciated, respected and recognized for my skills, knowledge and accomplishments on all levels now."*
	ESSENTIAL OILS	Bergamot, ***Cedarwood***, ***Frankincense***, ***Myrrh***, Sandalwood
	CRYSTALS	Red stones (element): Red Coral, Red Jade Yellow/Golden stones (chakra): Citrine, Gold Others: Carnelian, Elestial Crystal, Hematite, Malachite, Smoky Quartz, Tourmaline

CAUTION: Avoid essential oils listed in ***bold italic*** during pregnancy.

About the Attributes

Fame & Reputation is located at the back center 1/3 of your home (or Compass Direction: S)—where appreciation and recognition can enhance your reputation. Integrity of your actions also contributes to your reputation and can illuminate your life with good will among friends, co-workers and your community.

BAGUA MAP

Wealth & Prosperity	Fame & Reputation	Relationships, Love & Marriage
Family & Health	Tai Chi: Health & Unity	Creativity & Children
Knowledge & Self-Cultivation	Career	Helpful People & Travel

ENTRANCE
or COMPASS DIRECTION: S

The element related to Fame & Reputation is Fire. The triangular shape of the Fire element relates to the emotions and symbolizes outward movement. Its energetic qualities are expansive, passionate, sensual and social. This element relates to all life's passions, especially enthusiasm and vivaciousness.

The primary chakra associated with Fame & Reputation is the Crown Chakra, located at the top of the head. It is associated with the color violet. Consider: *Do you have the spiritual connection to aspire to your goals?*

The supporting chakra of this gua is the Solar Plexus Chakra, located between your navel and the bottom of the breastbone. It is associated with the color yellow. This is where you get that "gut feeling." Consider: *Are you using your personal power to control the integrity of your actions to attain a good reputation and fame?*

If you have any issues with this area of life, enhancing the Fame & Reputation area of your home and implementing the Make It Happen Process™ may help improve your well-being and attract what you want.

127

Feng Shui for Fame & Reputation

You can decorate with or use any combination of the following to enhance Fame & Reputation:

- **Colors** that are reds.

- **Shapes** of objects that look like a triangle, cone or pyramid.

- **Materials** that have or generate light including sunlight, lamps and candles. Items made of or appear to be made from animals such as feathers, wool and leather.

- **Artwork** including paintings, pictures and certificates of things that represent your accomplishments such as awards, diplomas, trophies or personal affirmation and inspirational sayings associated with Fame & Reputation.

TLC Process™ for Fame & Reputation

This method allows you to remove self-sabotage or "emotional blocks" using deprogramming or clearing statements, then reprogram with positive affirmations to better align yourself with your goals. Use the chart and workspace on the next page as idea starters for your personalized TLC Process™. For more details on this method, see Chapter 4.

FAME & REPUTATION
TLC Process

	DEPROGRAMMING (Clearing)	REPROGRAMMING (Affirmation)
TLC PROCESS STATEMENT	Tap on the side of your hand while saying your clearing statement 3 times: *"I deeply accept and love myself even though…*	Tap on top of your hand between the 4th and 5th knuckles while saying your affirmation statement *with feeling* 3 times: *"I totally and completely…*
	E X A M P L E S :	
…to Enhance LIFE GOALS	*…I falsely project to the world who I am."*	*…project to the world the person I truly am on all levels now."*
	…I lack appreciation, respect and recognition for my skills, knowledge and accomplishments."	*…am appreciated, respected and recognized for my skills, knowledge, and accomplishments on all levels now."*
	…I lack a good reputation with my colleagues and throughout my community."	*…attract and have a well-known, good reputation with my colleagues and throughout my community on all levels now."*

Deprogramming Your Negative Belief(s):

"I deeply accept and love myself even though _____

_____ *"*

Reprogramming Your Positive Belief(s) / Affirmation(s):

"I totally and completely _____

_____ *on all levels now."*

Aromatherapy for Fame & Reputation

Use a blend of any of the following essential oils with the intention of creating integrity of your action to enhance your good reputation and provide an opportunity for fame, if desired. For more information on essential oils, see Chapter 4.

Bergamot: Facilitates strength, power, confidence and motivation.

Cedarwood: Promotes self-control, self-image, confidence and power.
Caution: Avoid during pregnancy.

Frankincense: Facilitates wisdom, inspiration, performance and emotional stability. *Caution: Avoid during pregnancy.*

Myrrh: Uplifting. Facilitates spiritual awareness.
Caution: Avoid during pregnancy.

Sandalwood: Facilitates self-awareness, balance and connection. Facilitates joy, self-esteem and self-image. Helps to neutralize manipulation, obsession and aggression. Assists in calming and balancing the emotions.

Crystal Therapy for Fame & Reputation

Select a crystal that resonates with you and personalize it with your affirmation. Place the crystal over your written affirmation somewhere in this gua. For more information on crystals, see Chapter 4.

Use REDDISH crystals to represent the color associated with Fame & Reputation

Red Coral: Stimulates the energetic pursuits of goals.

Red Jade: Assists in the transformation of one's dreams into physical reality. Inspires ambition toward completion of objectives. Helps to release one's limitation and to actualize aspirations to achieve limitless achievements.

Use YELLOW-GOLDEN crystals to enhance the Solar Plexus Chakra, which supports Fame & Reputation

Citrine: Assist in business pursuits.

Gold: Attracts honors.

Other color crystals that can enhance Fame & Reputation

Carnelian: Stimulates inspiration.

Elestial Crystal: Enhances the power of personal expression and potential.

Hematite: Encourages one to reach for the stars.

Malachite: Assists in achieving desired goal.

Smoky Quartz: Helps you to achieve your highest aspirations and hopes.

Tourmaline: Attracts inspiration and self-confidence.

Feeling Unappreciated

Nancy was a 35-year-old actor and producer who wanted to be appreciated, respected and recognized for all that she did. She felt that her fellow colleagues negated her contributions, ignored her ideas and challenged her advice. She was not being called to audition for roles, hence, she was not being cast for any parts. As a seasoned actor, she was ready to be acknowledged once again for her talents.

Implementing the Make It Happen Process™

1) Nancy used the TLC Process™ for clearing the way to feel appreciated, respected and recognized.
   - *STEP A Deprogramming:*
   While tapping on the side of her hand, (see page 50), she repeated the following statement 3 times:

      "I deeply accept, love and honor myself even though I lack appreciation, respect and recognition on all levels now."

   - *STEP B Reprogramming with positive affirmation:*
   While tapping on the top of her hand (see page 51), she repeated the following statement 3 times:

      "I am appreciated, respected and recognized for all that I do on all levels now."

2) Nancy set her intentions by applying a blend of essential oils (see page 72) to the Fame & Reputation area of her home with a room spray and a body oil blend to the Crown and Solar Plexus chakras which support the Fame & Reputation area.

3) She then personalized and placed a red coral (see page 72) on top of her written affirmation in the Fame & Reputation area of her home.

The Results

Nancy was unexpectedly cast in a theatrical production to replace one of the actors who had to suddenly leave the production. She felt under-qualified and under-trained for the role. However, Nancy met the challenge head-on and was praised by her colleagues—and the media—for her performance. Nancy was praised repeatedly for her ability to successfully step in on such short notice, which made her feel appreciated, respected and recognized for the time, effort and talent she put toward the role. Fellow actors even remarked about how good Nancy smelled before each show!

Making News

As a business consultant, 28-year-old Sophia felt that her Fame and Reputation could always use more enhancement, and she would not mind a bit more recognition either. So she took matters into her own hands.

Implementing the Make It Happen Process™

1) Sophia applied the TLC Process™ for clearing the way to attract fame, reputation and recognition.

 - *STEP A Deprogramming:*
   While tapping on the side of her hand, (see page 50), she repeated the following statement 3 times:

   "I deeply accept, love and honor myself even though I lack fame, reputation and recognition on all levels now."

 - *STEP B Reprogramming with positive affirmation:*
   While tapping on the top of her hand (see page 51), she repeated the following statement 3 times:

   "I attract fame and reputation and am recognized for all that I do on all levels now."

2) Sophia set her intentions by applying a blend of essential oils (see page 72) to the Fame & Reputation area of her home with a room spray and a body oil blend for the Crown and Solar Plexus chakras which support the Fame & Reputation area.

3) She then personalized and placed a citrine (see page 72) on top of her written affirmation in the Fame & Reputation area of her home.

The Results

By the second day of starting the TLC Process™ and using the essential oils for Fame & Reputation, Sophia was contacted by a large newspaper to write an article on her business. Exactly the boost of fame and reputation she desired.

"Gravitation cannot be held responsible
for people falling in love."

— Albert Einstein

10 Deepen Your Relationships, Love & Marriage

The close relationships we form with others are a reflection of who we truly are. Being open to communication and intimacy can deepen the bond we have with significant people in our lives. Consider how well you attract healthy, loving relationships.

Checklist For When You Want To Enhance Relationships, Love & Marriage

Do you want to:

- ☐ Improve your current relationship?
- ☐ Attract a healthy and loving relationship into your life now?
- ☐ Improve your relationship with your co-workers or boss?

Do you feel that:

- ☐ You are in a relationship that allows you to fully express who you are?
- ☐ You are in a loving, intimate and healthy relationship?
- ☐ You allow your partner to fully express his/her own self unconditionally?
- ☐ You allow yourself to love and be loved?
- ☐ You attract an abundance of love and happiness in your life on all levels now?

If you would like to deepen your relationships, love and marriage, review the attributes and enhancements of this gua shown below, and apply the natural holistic methods discussed in this chapter.

RELATIONSHIPS, LOVE & MARRIAGE
Attributes & Enhancements

GUA ATTRIBUTES	ELEMENT	Earth
	COLOR	Pinks and Reds
	QUALITY	Receptivity
	CHAKRAS	Primary: Heart Supporting: Sacral
FENG SHUI ENHANCEMENTS	MUSICAL NOTES	Play music with the notes of F and D in this gua of your home.
	MATERIALS	Decorate with items that have pinks and soft reds; pairs of items that represent love and marriage, such as roses, rose quartz hearts, doves and mandarin ducks; mementos or gifts from a loved one that have romantic and loving associations with them.
	ARTWORK	Paintings and posters symbolizing love and romance, photos of yourself with your significant other, such as a wedding picture, or inspirational sayings associated with Relationships, Love & Marriage.
LIFE GOALS ENHANCEMENTS	TLC PROCESS Affirmation, such as:	*"I am in a loving, healthy and intimate relationship on all levels now."*
	ESSENTIAL OILS	Jasmine, Lavender, Neroli, Orange, Pine, Rose, Sandalwood, Ylang ylang
	CRYSTALS	Pink stones (element & chakra): Pink Tourmaline, Rhodocrosite, Rhodonite, Rose Quartz Green stones (chakra): Aventurine, Malachite Others: Citrine, Gold, Lapis lazuli, Ruby

About the Attributes

Relationships, Love & Marriage is located in the back right 1/3 corner of your home (or Compass Direction: SW)—where you can enhance loving relationships. Receptivity, the quality associated with this gua, is important in communication with one another for a loving relationship. Unconditional love, support, flexibility, adaptability, and devotion are other qualities associated with this area. All are important for happy, healthy and loving relationships.

The element related to Relationships, Love & Marriage is Earth. The Earth energy in this gua is that of Mother Earth, having the qualities of receptivity and nurturing. When one partner is receptive to the feelings and needs of the other, there is a nurturing environment. The pink color associated with this gua also brings in the Fire element, which can add some warmth and passion to a relationship or help to start one.

The primary chakra of this gua is the Heart Chakra, located over the center of your chest. It is associated with the color green. Consider: *Do you have feelings of unconditional love and support for each other for a happy, healthy relationship?*

The supporting chakra is the Sacral Chakra, located between the base of the spine and the navel. It is associated with the color orange. Consider: *This is where the emotion of feelings and the need for relationships are associated.*

If you have any issues with this area of life, enhancing the Relationships, Love & Marriage area of your home and implementing the Make It Happen Process™ may help improve your well-being and attract what you want.

BAGUA MAP

Wealth & Prosperity	Fame & Reputation	Relationships, Love & Marriage
Family & Health	Tai Chi: Health & Unity	Creativity & Children
Knowledge & Self-Cultivation	Career	Helpful People & Travel

ENTRANCE or COMPASS DIRECTION: SW

Feng Shui for Relationships, Love & Marriage

You can decorate with or use any combination of the following representations to enhance Relationships, Love & Marriage:

- **Colors** that are pinks and reds.

- **Pairs** of things that represent love and marriage, such as roses, rose quartz hearts and doves.

- **Materials,** mementos or gifts from a loved one that have romantic and loving associations with them.

- **Artwork** including paintings and posters symbolizing love and romance, photos of yourself with your significant other such as a wedding picture or inspirational quotes associated with Relationships, Love & Marriage.

TLC Process™ for Relationships, Love & Marriage

This method allows you to remove self-sabotage or "emotional blocks" using deprogramming or clearing statements, then reprogramming with positive affirmations to better align yourself with your goals. Use the chart and workspace on the next page as idea starters for your personalized TLC Process™. For more details on this method, see Chapter 4.

RELATIONSHIPS, LOVE & MARRIAGE
TLC Process

	DEPROGRAMMING (Clearing)	REPROGRAMMING (Affirmation)
TLC PROCESS STATEMENT...	Tap on the side of your hand while saying your clearing statement 3 times: *"I deeply accept and love myself even though...*	Tap on top of your hand between the 4th and 5th knuckles while saying your affirmation statement with feeling 3 times: *"I totally and completely...*
	EXAMPLES:	
...to Enhance LIFE GOALS	*...I lack a relationship that allows me to fully express who I am."*	*... am in a relationship that allows me to fully express who I am on all levels now."*
	...I lack a loving, healthy and intimate relationship."	*...am in a loving, healthy and intimate relationship on all levels now."*
	...I lack the ability to allow myself to love and be loved by others."	*...allow myself to love and be loved on all levels now."*

Deprogramming Your Negative Belief(s):

"I deeply accept and love myself even though _____."

Reprogramming Your Positive Belief(s)/Affirmation(s):

"I totally and completely _____ on all levels now."

Aromatherapy for Relationships, Love & Marriage

Use a blend of any of the following essential oils with the intention of creating a healthy, loving and joyful relationship and deeper romance with your partner. For more information on essential oils, see Chapter 4.

Jasmine: Acts as an aphrodisiac.

Lavender: Encourages compassion and love.

Neroli: Enhances sensuality. Facilitates peace and joy.

Orange: Uplifting, enhancing feelings of joy, contentment, happiness and light heartedness.

Pine: Facilitates forgiveness for self and others, acceptance of help, love and understanding. Reduces anxiety and rejuvenates the whole body.

Rose: Stimulating and uplifting, producing a feeling of well-being. Enhances feelings of harmony, forgiveness, love and compassion. Acts like an aphrodisiac.

Sandalwood: Facilitates self-awareness, balance, and connection. Facilitates joy, self-esteem and self-image. Facilitates balance, unity and healing. Helps to neutralize manipulation, obsession and aggression. Assists in calming and balancing the emotions.

Ylang ylang: Facilitates sensuality and sexuality. Assists in relationships. Acts as an aphrodisiac. Promotes feelings of peace, joy, self-love and confidence. Promotes unification. Reduces resentment, jealousy and frustration.

Crystal Therapy for Relationships, Love & Marriage

Select a crystal that resonates with you and personalize it with your affirmation. Place the crystal over your written affirmation somewhere in this gua. For more information on crystals, see Chapter 4.

Use PINK crystals to represent the color associated with Relationships, Love & Marriage

Pink Tourmaline: Joyfully receiving love and giving out love. Helps in healing matters of the heart.

Rhodocrosite: Known as a "stone of love and balance," it enhances love for self and others. Eases emotional pain.

Rhodonite: Known as a "stone of love," it resonates to unconditional love. Enhances self-worth, self-confidence and self-esteem.

Rose Quartz: As a "stone of gentle love," it enhances feelings and abilities to give and receive love and compassion, including self-love.

Use GREEN crystals to enhance the Heart Chakra, which supports Relationships, Love & Marriage

Aventurine: Aids in emotional stability.

Malachite: Represents loyalty in love, friendships and partnerships.

Other color crystals to enhance the Sacral Chakra, which supports Relationships, Love & Marriage

Citrine: Clears negativity.

Gold: Attracts cooperation and receptivity.

Lapis lazuli: Helps relationships be successful.

Ruby: Enhances feelings of love and compassion.

Finding Mr. Right

Elizabeth, a single mother with a pre-teen daughter, wanted to build a healthy intimate relationship with the right man. She had been dating for the last ten years, including two relationships that did not show much promise of a long-term future. About two years ago, Elizabeth decided that she would only date the "Right Guy" who would meet her most important qualifications—he had to love her daughter and accept and support her full and exciting life. However, since reaching that decision, she had not attracted one man in her life. No dates, no introductions, not even phone numbers!

Implementing the Make It Happen Process™

1) Elizabeth used the TLC Process™ for clearing her way to a healthy relationship.

- *STEP A Deprogramming:*
  While tapping on the side of her hand (see page 50), she repeated the following statement 3 times:

  "I deeply accept, love and honor myself even though I lack an intimate, healthy relationship on all levels now."

- *STEP B Reprogramming with positive affirmation:*
  While tapping on the top of her hand (see page 51), she repeated the following statement 3 times:

  "I attract and have an intimate, healthy relationship with my dynamic life partner now, who has the qualities I want on all levels now."

2) Elizabeth set her intentions by applying a blend of essential oils (see page 73) to the Relationships, Love & Marriage area of her home with a room spray and a body oil to her Heart and Sacral Chakras with the intention of meeting "Mr. Right."

3) She then personalized and placed two rose quartz crystal hearts (see page 73) in the Relationships, Love & Marriage area of her home.

The Results

Within two days of implementing the program, Elizabeth was approached by a man who possessed all the qualities she wanted. They had met casually through mutual friends about a year prior. He had kept up on her, amazed and impressed with her adventures. Once he took the first step, they made a romantic connection. They have since formed a dynamic, passionate relationship that also includes business partnerships, travel and loving family support.

Missing My Sweetheart

Sean and Morgan, a married couple, were both so busy with their careers, they found it difficult to spend time together. Sean worked at night and Morgan worked during the day. The one day a week they both had off was not spent together, as each went about his or her own activities. Sean and Morgan wanted more quality time with each other.

Implementing the Make It Happen Process™

1) Sean and Morgan applied the TLC Process™ for clearing the way to find quality time to be together.

- *STEP A Deprogramming:*

  While tapping on the side of their hands (see page 50), Sean and Morgan repeated the following statement 3 times:

  "I deeply accept, love and honor myself even though we lack quality time to be together on all levels now."

- *STEP B Reprogramming with positive affirmation:*

  While tapping on the top of their hands (see page 51), Sean and Morgan repeated the following statement 3 times:

  "We find time to be together and spend quality time with each other on all levels now."

2) Sean and Morgan applied a blend of essential oils (see page 73) to the Relationships, Love & Marriage area of their home with a room spray and a body oil blend to the Heart and Sacral Chakras which support the Relationships, Love & Marriage area.

3) Sean and Morgan then personalized and placed a rose quartz (see page 73) on top of their written affirmation in the Love & Marriage area of their home.

The Results

To their amazement, Sean's work schedule was changed from a night to day shift. Morgan was delighted that they now had the evenings to spend together. They have also designated Sundays as their time for daytime dates. As an added bonus, Morgan was pleasantly surprised that Sean started helping around the house!

"All children are artists.
The problem is how to remain
an artist once he grows up."

—Pablo Picasso

11 Nurture Your Creativity & Children

Youth can be a time of unbridled creativity and joy. Being in touch with this aspect of life makes us free to express ideas, problem solve and enjoy life to the fullest. How would your life improve by nurturing your own creativity and relationship with your children?

Checklist For When You Want To Enhance Creativity & Children

Do you want to:

- ☐ Increase your creativity?
- ☐ Improve your relationship with your children?
- ☐ Bring joy into your life?

Do you feel that:

- ☐ You allow your creativity to be fully expressed easily with joy?
- ☐ You allow time for yourself to express your creativity through design, art and projects?
- ☐ You allow your children to fully express themselves in a safe environment and love them unconditionally?

If you would like to nurture your creativity and relationship with your children, review the attributes and enhancements of this gua shown below, and apply the natural holistic methods discussed in this chapter.

CREATIVITY & CHILDREN
Attributes & Enhancements

GUA ATTRIBUTES	ELEMENT	Metal
	COLOR	White and Pastels
	QUALITY	Integrity
	CHAKRAS	Primary: Sacral Supporting: Throat and Heart
FENG SHUI ENHANCEMENTS	MUSICAL NOTES	Play music with the notes of D, G and F in this gua of your home.
	MATERIALS	Decorate with items that are white, pastel, oval, round or have an arch shape. Items made of metal, natural crystals and gemstones.
	ARTWORK	Paintings, photos, posters and sculptures of children or symbolizing creativity and joy. Anything made by children. Personal affirmations and inspirational sayings about Creativity & Children.
LIFE GOALS ENHANCEMENTS	TLC PROCESS Affirmations, such as:	*"I allow my creativity to be fully expressed easily with joy on all levels now."*
	ESSENTIAL OILS	Bergamot, Chamomile, Roman, Cypress, Geranium, Lavender, Mandarin, Orange, Pine, Rosewood, Sandalwood, Tangerine, Ylang ylang
	CRYSTALS	White, Pastel or Metal stones (element): Amazonite, Aventurine, Gold, Pink Tourmaline, Smoky Quartz Orange stones (chakra): Carnelian, Citrine Other stones: Azurite, Black Obsidian, Bloodstone, Diamond, Emerald, Garnet, Malachite, Sodalite, Tiger Eye

About the Attributes

Creativity & Children is located in the middle right 1/3 of your home (or Compass Direction: W)—where creativity and youthful joy thrive. Joy is the quality associated with this gua, as well as encouragement, generosity and pleasure. When this area is enhanced, children can learn and grow joyfully through creative expression. Your own creativity can thrive, too.

The element associated with Creativity & Children is Metal. The Metal element is symbolized by ores, salts, minerals and crystals (gemstones). The round/oval shape of the Metal element relates to the Intellect and symbolizes inward movement. Its energetic qualities are mentally clear, logical, precise and focused. It relates to organization, structure, and being law abiding and safety-conscious.

BAGUA MAP

Wealth & Prosperity	Fame & Reputation	Relationships, Love & Marriage
Family & Health	Tai Chi: Health & Unity	Creativity & Children
Knowledge & Self-Cultivation	Career	Helpful People & Travel

ENTRANCE
or COMPASS DIRECTION: W

The primary chakra for this gua is the Sacral Chakra, located between the base of the spine and the navel. It is associated with the color orange. Consider: *This chakra is associated with creativity and where children are conceived.*

Additionally, there are two supporting chakras: Throat and Heart. The Throat Chakra is located at the throat and is associated with the color blue. Consider: *Does your environment allow children and creativity to express themselves freely?* The Heart Chakra is located over the center of your chest and is associated with the color green. Consider: *Is there a loving environment where creativity and children can thrive joyfully?*

If you have any issues with this area of life, enhancing the Creativity & Children area and implementing the Make It Happen Process™ may help improve your well-being and attract what you want.

Feng Shui for Creativity & Children

You can decorate with or use any combination of the following to enhance the Creativity & Children area:

- **Colors** that are white or pastels.

- **Shapes** of objects that are oval, round or have an arch.

- **Materials** made of metal such as brass and silver. Also natural crystals and gemstones.

- **Artwork** including paintings, photos, posters and sculptures of children or symbolizing creativity and joy. Anything made by children. Personal affirmations or inspirational sayings about Creativity & Children.

TLC Process™ for Creativity & Children

This method allows you to remove self-sabotage or "emotional blocks" using deprogramming or clearing statements, then reprogram with positive affirmations to better align yourself with your goals. Use the chart and workspace on the next page as idea starters for your personalized TLC Process™. For more details on this method, see Chapter 4.

CREATIVITY & CHILDREN
TLC Process

	DEPROGRAMMING (Clearing)	REPROGRAMMING (Affirmation)
TLC PROCESS STATEMENT...	Tap on the side of your hand while saying your clearing statement 3 times: *"I deeply accept and love myself even though...*	Tap on top of your hand between the 4th and 5th knuckles while saying your affirmation statement *with feeling* 3 times: *"I totally and completely...*
	E X A M P L E S :	
...to Enhance LIFE GOALS	*...I lack the ability to express my creativity easily and joyfully."*	*...allow my creativity to be fully expressed easily with joy on all levels now."*
	...I lack time for myself to express my creativity through design, art and projects."	*...allow time for myself to express my creativity through design, art and projects on all levels now."*
	...I prevent my children to fully express themselves in a safe environment."	*...allow my children to fully express themselves in a safe environment and love them unconditionally on all levels now."*

Deprogramming Your Negative Belief(s):

"I deeply accept and love myself even though _____

_____ ."

Reprogramming Your Positive Belief(s) / Affirmation(s):

"I totally and completely _____

_____ *on all levels now."*

153

Aromatherapy for Creativity & Children

Use a blend of any of the following oils with the intention of bringing out your inner child and sense of joy and creativity, as well as enhancing your relationship with your children. For more information on essential oils, see Chapter 4.

Bergamot: Facilitates strength, power, confidence, and motivation. Relieves feelings of anxiety, stress and tension.

Chamomile, Roman: Facilitates peace, joy and relaxation. Balances the emotions.

Cypress: Produces a feeling of grounding and security. Facilitates confidence, strength and courage.

Geranium: Facilitates creativity, security and balance. Promotes feelings of well-being and peace. Uplifting and assists in stabilizing the emotions.

Lavender: Promotes relaxation, calmness and emotional/physical balancing. Encourages health, inner peace, compassion and love.

Mandarin: Uplifts, revitalizes and refreshes. Facilitates happiness.

Orange: Uplifting, enhancing feelings of joy, contentment, happiness and lightheartedness.

Pine: Facilitates forgiveness for self and others, acceptance of help, love and understanding. Reduces anxiety and rejuvenates the whole body.

Rosewood: Produces a sense of relaxation and peace.

Sandalwood: Facilitates self-awareness, balance and connection. Facilitates joy, self-esteem and self-image. Facilitates balance, unity and healing. Helps to neutralize manipulation, obsession and aggression. Assists in calming and balancing the emotions.

Tangerine: Promotes a sense of calmness, reducing anxiety.

Ylang ylang: Promotes feelings of peace, joy, self-love and confidence. Promotes unification. Reduces resentment, jealousy and frustration.

Crystal Therapy for Creativity & Children

Select a crystal that resonates with you and personalize it with your affirmation. Place the crystal over your written affirmation somewhere in this gua. For more information on crystals, see Chapter 4.

Use PASTEL or METAL crystals to represent the color and Metal element associated with Creativity & Children

Amazonite: Enhances communication related to love.

Aventurine: Enhances creativity and motivation in activities.

Gold: Attracts cooperation and receptivity.

Pink Tourmaline: Promotes creativity. Encourages feelings of peace and joy during times of change and growth. Receives and gives love joyfully.

Smoky Quartz: Enhances joy of living, helps regulate creativity in business.

Use ORANGE crystals to enhance the Sacral Chakra, which supports Creativity & Children

Carnelian: Enhances creativity and compassion.

Citrine: Stimulates intuition and creativity.

Other color crystals that can enhance Creativity & Children

Azurite: Enhances creativity and compassion.

Black Obsidian: Induces creativity in all activities.

Bloodstone: Enhances creativity.

Diamond: Inspires imagination, inventiveness and creativity.

Emerald: Enhances creativity and speech.

Garnet: Assists creative powers into manifestation.

Malachite: Protects your creative ideas.

Sodalite: Enhance truthfulness in emotions, allowing one to recognize and express true feelings.

Tiger Eye: Enhances creativity and practical decision-making.

155

Bored At Work

Ann found her job as a teacher boring and mundane. She dreaded going to work every day. Ann wanted to feel more joy and creativity in teaching the same material year after year.

Implementing the Make It Happen Process

1) Ann used the TLC Process™ for clearing the way to find creativity and joy in her work.

- *STEP A Deprogramming:*
  While tapping on the side of her hand, (see page 50), she repeated the following statement 3 times:

   "I deeply accept, love and honor myself even though I lack creativity and joy in my work on all levels now."

- *STEP B Reprogramming with positive affirmation:*
  While tapping on the top of her hand (see page 51), she repeated the following statement 3 times:

   "I find creativity and joy in my work on all levels now."

2) Then Ann set her intentions by applying a blend of essential oils (see page 73) to the Creativity & Children area of her home with a room spray and body oil to the Sacral Chakra to enhance creativity, and the Heart Chakra to enhance joy for her career.

3) Ann then personalized and placed a citrine crystal (see page 73) over her written affirmation in the Creativity & Children area of her home.

The Results

Ann now finds that her students are a joy to teach. She looks forward to going to work and has even found new creative ways to teach her same lessons.

The Art of Parenting

Joyce was a mother of two young children in elementary school and owned her own business. She found herself so busy with her career that she had little time to enjoy her kids and her long-time creative passion—painting. Joyce turned to the Make It Happen Process to help her address these two issues.

Implementing the Make It Happen Process

1) Joyce used the TLC Process™ for clearing the way to find joy and time to be with her children and to allow her creativity to flow in her artwork.

- *STEP A Deprogramming:*
  While tapping on the side of her hand, (see page 50), she repeated the following statement 3 times:

  "I deeply accept, love and honor myself even though I lack joyful times to be with my children and block my creativity in my artwork on all levels now."

- *STEP B Reprogramming with positive affirmation:*
  While tapping on the top of her hand (see page 51), she repeated the following statement 3 times:

  "I find joy and time to be with my children and allow my creativity to flow in my artwork on all levels now."

2) Joyce set her intentions by applying a blend of essential oils (see page 73) to the Creativity & Children area of her home with a room spray and body oil to the sacral chakra to enhance creativity for her artwork, and the Heart Chakra to enhance joy for being with her children.

3) Joyce then personalized and placed a citrine crystal (see page 73) over her written affirmation in the Creativity & Children area of her home.

The Results

After Joyce began using the Make It Happen Process, finding time to spend with her children came easily. Joyce also noticed that when she sat down to paint, her creativity flowed with ease.

"The World is a great mirror.
It reflects back to you what you are.
If you are loving, if you are friendly,
if you are helpful,
the World will prove loving and friendly
and helpful to you.
The World is what you are."

—Thomas Dreier

12 Discover Helpful People & Travel

Being at the right place at the right time, a concept known as *synchronicity*, aligns us with the people and opportunities that can bring us good fortune. Do you have the resources to take you to all the places you want to go in life?

Checklist For When You Want To Enhance Helpful People & Travel

Do you want to:

- ❏ Attract helpful people in your career or personal life, such as mentors, colleagues and clients?
- ❏ Have synchronicity and good fortune in your life?
- ❏ Change the location of your home or business?
- ❏ Enjoy new travel opportunities?

Do you feel that:

- ❏ You attract and are surrounded by generous and loving helpful people both in your personal and business life?
- ❏ Your life easily flows with synchronicity?
- ❏ You are in the right place at the right time to meet the right people who can be helpful in your life?

If you would like to bring synchronicity for good fortune and travel into your life, review the attributes and enhancements of this gua shown below, and apply the natural holistic methods discussed in this chapter.

HELPFUL PEOPLE & TRAVEL
Attributes & Enhancements

GUA ATTRIBUTES	ELEMENT	Metal
	COLOR	Grays
	QUALITY	Synchronicity
	CHAKRAS	Primary: Throat Supporting: Third Eye
FENG SHUI ENHANCEMENTS	MUSICAL NOTES	Play music with the notes of G and A in this gua of your home.
	MATERIALS	Decorate with items that are gray, oval, round or have an arch shape. Items made of metal, natural crystals and gemstones.
	ARTWORK	Paintings, photos, and posters of people who are helpful to you or of places you want to travel. Personal affirmations and inspirational sayings about Helpful People & Travel.
LIFE GOALS ENHANCEMENTS	TLC PROCESS Affirmations, such as:	*"I allow my life to flow easily with synchronicity and good fortune on all levels now."*
	ESSENTIAL OILS	Lavender, Lemon, ***Peppermint***, Pine, Rosewood
	CRYSTALS	Gray or Metal stones (element): Clear Quartz, Elestial Crystal Blue stones (chakra): Aquamarine, Celestite, Sapphire, Turquoise Other stones: Aventurine

CAUTION: Avoid essential oils listed in ***bold italic*** during pregnancy.

About the Attributes

Helpful People & Travel is located in the front right 1/3 corner of your home (or Compass Direction: NW)—where being at the right place at the right time can enhance your good fortune. Synchronicity is the quality associated with this gua, in which all aspects of your life flow easily and as you desire. Inspiration, confidence and power are also qualities that are associated with this area.

BAGUA MAP

Wealth & Prosperity	Fame & Reputation	Relationships, Love & Marriage
Family & Health	Tai Chi: Health & Unity	Creativity & Children
Knowledge & Self-Cultivation	Career	Helpful People & Travel

ENTRANCE
or COMPASS DIRECTION: NW

The element associated with Helpful People & Travel is Metal. The Metal element is symbolized by ores, salts, minerals and crystals (gemstones). The round/oval shape of the Metal element relates to the Intellect and symbolizes inward movement. Its energetic qualities are mentally clear, logical, precise and focused. This shape relates to organization, structure, and being law abiding and safety-conscious.

The primary chakra in this gua is the Throat Chakra. It is located at your throat and is associated with the color blue. Consider: Are you able to communicate clearly with the helpful people or benefactors in your life?

The supporting chakra is the Third Eye Chakra, located at the center of the forehead between the brows. It is associated with the color of indigo. Consider: *Are you able to connect with helpful people of higher consciousness?*

Your Third Eye Chakra also is connected to your pineal gland, which is responsible for timing. Consider: *Are you in the right place at the right time to attract the right helpful people in your life?*

If you have any issues with this area of life, enhancing the Helpful People & Travel area and implementing the Make It Happen Process™ may help improve your well-being and attract what you want.

Feng Shui for Helpful People & Travel

You can decorate with or use any of the following representations to bring in the Metal element to enhance Helpful People & Travel.

- **Colors** that are any shade of gray.

- **Shapes** of objects that are oval, round or have an arch.

- **Materials** that are made of metal and natural crystals and gemstones.

- **Artwork** such as paintings, photos, and posters of people who are helpful to you in both your business and personal life physically, such as mentors, colleagues, friends and family and spiritually such as angels and spiritual teachers. Also artwork of places you want to travel and visit. Personal affirmations or inspirational quotes associated with Helpful People & Travel.

TLC Process™ for Helpful People & Travel

This method allows you to remove self-sabotage or "emotional blocks" using deprogramming or clearing statements, then reprogram with positive affirmations to better align yourself with your goals. Use the chart and workspace on the next page as idea starters for your personalized TLC Process™. For more details on this method, see Chapter 4.

HELPFUL PEOPLE & TRAVEL
TLC Process

	DEPROGRAMMING (Clearing)	REPROGRAMMING (Affirmation)
TLC PROCESS STATEMENT...	Tap on the side of your hand while saying your clearing statement 3 times: **"I deeply accept and love myself even though...**	Tap on top of your hand between the 4th and 5th knuckles while saying your affirmation statement *with feeling* 3 times: **"I totally and completely...**
	EXAMPLES:	
...to Enhance LIFE GOALS	...I lack synchronicity and good fortune in my life."	...allow my life to flow easily with synchronicity and good fortune on all levels now."
	...I lack the timing to be in the right place at the right time to meet the right people that are helpful in my life."	...I am in the right place at the right time to meet the right people who are helpful in my life on all levels now."
	...I lack the opportunity to travel where and when I want to."	...I am able to travel where I want and when I want to on all levels now."

Deprogramming Your Negative Belief(s):

"I deeply accept and love myself even though _____

_____ ."

Reprogramming Your Positive Belief(s)/Affirmation(s):

"I totally and completely _____

_____ *on all levels now."*

Aromatherapy for Helpful People & Travel

Use a blend of any of the following oils with the intention of enhancing synchronicity of events, helping you to be in the right place with the right people at the right time, thus bringing you good fortune; as well as the opportunity to travel, if you wish. For more information on essential oils, see Chapter 4.

Lavender: Facilitates acceptance and assistance.

Lemon: Encourages communication and acceptance of help.

Peppermint: Promotes acceptance and communication.
  Caution: Avoid during pregnancy.

Pine: Facilitates acceptance of help, love and understanding.

Rosewood: Produces a sense of relaxation and peace.

Crystal Therapy for Helpful People & Travel

Select a crystal that resonates with you and personalize it with your affirmation. Place the crystal over your written affirmation somewhere in this gua. For more information on crystals, see Chapter 4.

Use GRAY or METAL gemstones to represent the color and Metal element associated with Helpful People & Travel

Clear Quartz: As a "stone of power," it facilitates communication with the helpful people in your life, such as spiritual masters, teachers and healers.

Elestial Crystals: Assists in bringing the heart and the intellect into synchronicity and aligning with the spiritual realm.

Use BLUE gemstones to enhance the Throat Chakra, which supports Helpful People & Travel

Aquamarine: Facilitates higher levels of communication.

Celestite: Aids in ease of communication.

Sapphire: Assists in communication.

Turquoise: Enhances communication skills. Thought to provide protection during travel against accidents.

Other color crystals that can enhance Helpful People & Travel

Aventurine: Enhances opportunity and good luck.

Opportunity Knocks

Linda, a 28-year-old woman, was finding it difficult to attract the right business mentors and other people in her life who could help further her career. She felt stuck, alone and without the support she needed to succeed.

Implementing the Make It Happen Process™

1) *Linda used the TLC Process™ for clearing the way to be in the right place at the right time to achieve her personal and business goals.*

   - *STEP A Deprogramming:*
     While tapping on the side of her hand, (see page 50), she repeated the following statement 3 times:

     "I deeply accept, love and honor myself even though I miss opportunities to achieve my personal and business goals on all levels now."

   - *STEP B Reprogramming with positive affirmation:*
     While tapping on the top of her hand (see page 51), she repeated the following statement 3 times:

     "May I be in the right place, at the right time, and the right people placed in my path so that I may achieve my personal and business goals on all levels now."

2) *Linda also set her intentions by applying the appropriate essential oils (see page 73) for the Helpful People & Travel area of her home three times a day for over a month. During this time, new and old business contacts started calling and booking appointments with her. After attending a networking event, Linda was offered an opportunity that she greatly desired and had not considered possible. She explains, "I was in the right place, at the right time, and the right people were in my path to make it all come together. That unexpected opportunity has made it possible to grow and expand my business even more and to bring a higher level of expertise to my profession."*

Investment Paid Off

Speros and Lana had invested $100,000 in a restaurant with a business partner. They soon discovered the partner was stealing the profits and obviously lacked integrity to run the business. They wanted out and requested their investment back. The partner refused and the case went to court.

Speros and Lana set their intentions by applying a blend of essential oils (see page 73) to their home and bodies. They also personalized an aventurine crystal (see page 73) with the intention of getting their full investment back and placed it in the Helpful People & Travel area of their home.

Within a few months, the partner decided to settle out of court and return their full investment. Although delighted and relieved at this turn of events, Speros and Lana are still dumfounded to this day about the business partner's sudden change of heart.

"When there is light in the soul,
there is beauty in the person;

When there is beauty in the person,
there is harmony in the home;

When there is harmony in the home,
there is honor in the nation;

When there is honor in the nation,
there is peace in the world."

—Old Chinese proverb

13 Promote Tai Chi: Health & Unity

When all aspects of our life are in order, we feel centered, complete and grounded. The Tai Chi, or center of the home, unites all these aspects (guas), reflecting the wellness of our physical, emotional and spiritual health. Consider how you are promoting health and unity in your life.

Checklist For When You Want To Enhance Tai Chi: Health & Unity

Do you want to:

- ☐ Optimize your health?
- ☐ Recover from an illness?
- ☐ Feel and be grounded?

Do you feel that:

- ☐ You have balance and harmony in all aspects of life?
- ☐ You are whole and grounded in your life?
- ☐ You are able to handle stress well and therefore, have optimum health?

If you would like to promote health and a sense of unity and being grounded in your life, review the attributes and enhancements of this gua shown below, and apply the natural holistic methods discussed in this chapter.

TAI CHI: HEALTH & UNITY
Attributes & Enhancements

GUA ATTRIBUTES	ELEMENT	Earth
	COLOR	Earthtones and Yellows
	QUALITY	Unity (Harmony)
	CHAKRAS	Primary: Solar Plexus, Heart
FENG SHUI ENHANCEMENTS	MUSICAL NOTES	Play music with the notes of E and F in this gua of your home.
	MATERIALS	Decorate with items that have earthtone colors, or square/rectangular in shape. Items made of the earth such as tile, brick and ceramic.
	ARTWORK	Paintings, photos and posters showing or incorporating any of the above qualities. Any ceramic vases and artwork. Personal affirmations and inspirational sayings about unity, health and harmony.
LIFE GOALS ENHANCEMENTS	TLC PROCESS Affirmation, such as:	*"I am grounded and have balance and harmony in all aspects of my life on all levels now."*
	ESSENTIAL OILS	Eucalyptus globulus, Geranium, ***Juniper***, Lavender, Sandalwood, Spruce, Ylang ylang
	CRYSTALS	Golden stones (chakra and element): Amber (golden), Citrine, Tiger Eye Green stones (chakra): Aventurine, Jade Other stones: Carnelian, Celestite, Diamond, Flourite, Hematite, Clear Quartz, Rose Quartz

CAUTION: Avoid essential oils listed in ***bold italic*** during pregnancy.

About the Attributes

Tai Chi: Health & Unity is located at the Center of your home. Much like the hub of a wheel, the center of the home represents all aspects of your life coming together as one to create harmony and balance. This unity is the main quality associated with this gua. It makes the home feel whole and grounded, and can help you achieve optimum health. By minimizing stress in all aspects of your life and allowing your mind and body to be at peace, you can enhance your well-being.

BAGUA MAP

Wealth & Prosperity	Fame & Reputation	Relationships, Love & Marriage
Family & Health	Tai Chi: Health & Unity	Creativity & Children
Knowledge & Self-Cultivation	Career	Helpful People & Travel

ENTRANCE
or COMPASS DIRECTION: Center

The element related to this gua is Earth, which is symbolized by the ground, dirt and soil. The square/rectangle shape of the Earth element symbolizes stabilization. Its energetic qualities are grounding, nurturing and comforting.

The chakras of the Tai Chi: Health & Unity gua are the Solar Plexus and Heart Chakras. Located between the navel and bottom of the breastbone, the Solar Plexus Chakras is where you get that "gut feeling." The golden yellow color associated with this chakra represents the Earth element for the center of the house. Likewise, the Earth element is associated with the stomach, pancreas and spleen. Consider: *How do you digest the different areas of your life? Do you have enough "sweetness" and joy in your life? Do you accept and love yourself?*

The Heart Chakra is located over your heart center. Likewise, the "heart" of the house is associated with the Center of the home. Consider: *Do you circulate love and joy in all aspects of your life, including career, family and relationships with your significant other and children?*

If you have any issues with this area of life, enhancing the Tai Chi: Health & Unity area and implementing the Make It Happen Process™ may help improve your well-being and sense of unity.

Feng Shui for Tai Chi: Health & Unity

You can decorate with or use any of the following representations to enhance Tai Chi: Health & Unity:

- **Colors** that are earthtones, such as beige and yellow.

- **Shapes** of objects that are square and rectangular.

- **Materials** that are made of the earth, such as tile, brick and ceramic items.

- **Artwork** such as paintings, photos and posters showing or incorporating any of the above qualities. Any ceramic vases and artwork. Personal affirmations and inspirational sayings about unity, health and harmony.

TLC Process™ for Tai Chi: Health & Unity

This method allows you to remove self-sabotage or "emotional blocks" using deprogramming or clearing statements, then reprogram with positive affirmations to better align yourself with your goals. Use the chart and workspace on the next page as idea starters for your personalized TLC Process™. For more details on this method, see Chapter 4.

TAI CHI: HEALTH & UNITY
TLC Process

	DEPROGRAMMING (Clearing)	REPROGRAMMING (Affirmation)
TLC PROCESS STATEMENT...	Tap on the side of your hand while saying your clearing statement 3 times: *"I deeply accept and love myself even though...*	Tap on top of your hand between the 4th and 5th knuckles while saying your affirmation statement *with feeling* 3 times: *"I totally and completely...*
	EXAMPLES:	
...to Enhance LIFE GOALS	*...I lack balance and harmony in all aspects of my life."*	*...have balance and harmony in all aspects of my life on all levels now."*
	...I lack the feeling of being whole and grounded in my life."	*...feel whole and grounded in my life on all levels now."*
	...I lack the ability to handle stress and therefore have a state of dis-ease and compromised health."	*...am able to handle stress well and therefore have a state of ease and optimum health on all levels now."*

Deprogramming Your Negative Belief(s):

"I deeply accept and love myself even though _____

_____ *."*

Reprogramming Your Positive Belief(s)/Affirmation(s):

"I totally and completely _____

_____ *on all levels now."*

177

Aromatherapy for Tai Chi: Health & Unity

Use a blend of any of the following essential oils with the intention of creating health, harmony and unity so that all aspects of your life may become grounded, enhancing optimal health for all in your home. For more information on essential oils, see Chapter 4.

Eucalyptus globulus: Supports and encourages purification, health and well-being.

Geranium: Facilitates creativity, security and balance. Promotes feelings of well-being and peace. Uplifting and assists in stabilizing the emotions.

Juniper: Induces feelings of peace, love and health.
Caution: Avoid during pregnancy.

Lavender: Promotes relaxation, calmness and emotional/physical balancing. Encourages health, inner peace, compassion and love. Promotes a sense of well-being.

Sandalwood: Facilitates self-awareness, balance and connection. Facilitates joy, self-esteem and self-image. Facilitates balance, unity and healing. Helps to neutralize manipulation, obsession and aggression. Assists in calming and balancing the emotions.

Spruce: Grounding, produces the feeling of balance.

Ylang ylang: Promotes feelings of peace, joy, self-love and confidence. Promotes unification. Reduces resentment, jealousy and frustration.

Crystal Therapy for Tai Chi: Health & Unity

Select a crystal that resonates with you and personalize it with your affirmation. Place the crystal on top of your written affirmation somewhere in this gua. For more information on crystals, see Chapter 4.

Use YELLOW or GOLD crystals to represent the color and the Earth element and to enhance the Solar Plexus Chakra which supports Tai Chi: Health & Unity

Amber, golden: Provides grounding and protection.

Citrine: Helps to smooth over group and family problems thus producing cohesiveness within that group.

Tiger Eye: Balances the yin and yang energies.

Use GREEN crystals to enhance the Heart Chakra, which supports Tai Chi: Health & Unity

Aventurine: Assists in balancing the yin and yang energies.

Jade: Known as a "stone of harmony," it facilitates peace between the emotional, mental and physical.

Other color crystals to enhance Tai Chi: Health & Unity

Carnelian: Helps to stabilize the energy in the home.

Celestite: Balances the yin and yang energies. Attracts harmony and calmness.

Diamond: Brings harmony to all aspects of one's life.

Flourite: As a "stone of discernment," it discourages chaos and disruption. Enhances the perfect ideal of health and emotional well-being.

Hematite: Helps balance the body, mind, spirit, and yin and yang energies. Provides a state of mind that allows grounding, harmony and emotional clarity.

Quartz, clear: Has a natural tendency for harmony.

Rose Quartz: Balances the yin and yang energies.

Better Back

Roger was a 60-year-old man with lower back problems. He had been seeing a chiropractor for years with no relief. Holistically, the lower back represents the foundation for the body and is associated with finances and family. Interestingly, he was worried about having enough money for retirement even though he was already financially stable.

Implementing the Make It Happen Process™

1) *Roger did the TLC Process™ for clearing the way to be financially stable and have a strong foundation for his family and health.*

   • *STEP A Deprogramming:*
   While tapping on the side of his hand, (see page 50), he repeated the following statement 3 times:

   > **"I deeply accept, love and honor myself even though I lack a strong foundation for finances, family and health on all levels now."**

   • *STEP B Reprogramming with positive affirmation:*
   While tapping on the top of his hand (see page 51), he repeated the following statement 3 times:

   > **"I am financially stable and have a strong foundation in my family and health on all levels now."**

2) *Roger set his intentions by applying used a blend of essential oils (see page 73) in a room spray for the Tai Chi: Health & Unity area of his home.*

The Results

Roger followed up on his affirmation for two weeks. Within that time, his back felt better, and now he does not have to see the chiropractor as often. His quality of life has improved and he can enjoy his time with his grandchildren even more!

Stairway to Heaven

Mary, 59, had been struggling with knee problems for years. She found it difficult to walk fast or go up stairs. Mary wanted to increase her mobility and overall health. Holistically, the knees are associated with moving forward in life, so the Make It Happen Process™ was a natural solution for her. It is interesting to note that she was also pondering new career choices and felt "stuck."

Implementing the Make It Happen Process™

1) Mary applied the TLC Process™ for clearing the way to be able to move forward in her life.

- *STEP A Deprogramming:*

  While tapping on the side of her hand, (see page 50), she repeated the following statement 3 times:

  "I deeply accept, love and honor myself even though I am unable to move forward in my life on all levels now."

- *STEP B Reprogramming with positive affirmation:*

  While tapping on the top of her hand (see page 51), she repeated the following statement 3 times:

  " I look forward to moving forward in my life on all levels now."

2) Mary also set her intentions by applying a blend of essential oils (see page 73) to the Tai Chi: Health & Unity area of her home with a room spray and a body oil to her Heart and Solar Plexus Chakras to support this aspect of her home and life.

The Results

Shortly after implementing the Make It Happen Process™, Mary went on vacation where she encountered many steps. Much to her surprise, she noticed that climbing the stairs was both effortless and painless. Her knees supported her well, allowing her to move forward, on her literal and figurative journey, with ease. Mary enjoyed the "heavenly" results. Since then, she has also chosen her new career and is taking the steps necessary to reach her goal.

"There is only one success—
to spend your life in your own way."

—Christopher Morley

14 More Success Stories— Real People, Real Results, Really Amazing!

In this chapter you will read about some of the successes, big and small, that people of all ages and walks of life have enjoyed by applying essential oils, an effective Feng Shui tool, to enhance certain aspects of their life. In these examples, the individuals applied my own blends of *Jewel Essence*® Feng Shui Aromatherapy which I was inspired to develop based on my research for this book. These products are available to order online via my website. Also, see the product information page at the end of this book.

However, you also can make your own blends. Find the chapter in this book that relates to a specific gua you want to enhance. Then select essential oils that resonate with you and use as suggested in this book. You can add distilled water to the oils to create a room spray, or add carrier oils such as grapeseed and jojoba to make a body oil which you can apply to the appropriate chakra(s).

If you find success in your own quest to enhance an area of your life by applying the techniques I have discussed in this book, I would love to hear about it. You can share your success story with me via e-mail: info@JenLeong.com.

The stories that follow could very well motivate you to attract what you want… make it happen!

Businesses owners, Doug and Lyn, were in the midst of a lawsuit filed by an employee when they contacted me for a Feng Shui consultation. The lawsuit had been dragging on for several years and they wanted it to end quickly, in their favor. I made recommendations for creating more harmony and balance in their home and enhancing the Helpful People & Travel area. I also suggested that they use "Jewel Essence® of Synchronicity" to attract the right people at the right time that would help settle the lawsuit in their favor, as well as "Jewel Essence® of Recognition" to enhance their good integrity and reputation. I also had Lyn write an affirmation of the desired outcome of their lawsuit. Lyn used the Feng Shui aromatherapy diligently and it paid off—the court ruled in favor of the company and the employee now owes the company money instead!

* * *

Girl Scout Troop 8472 was in the middle of their annual Girl Scout cookie fund-raiser. My daughter, Krystal, was a member of the troop so I suggested the girls use essential oils for prosperity to increase sales at their site sale location outside the grocery store. The scouts sprayed "Jewel Essence® of Prosperity" aromatherapy mist on themselves and around the cookie display table. In previous years, sales at similar times and locations averaged about 35 boxes per session. This time, however, they increased sales by approximately 64 percent, selling about 55 boxes, much to the delight of the Scouts, their parents and troop leaders!

* * *

John owned a business that had potential, but it was draining money. He had tried to sell the business for more than a year without luck. He used "Jewel Essence® of Success" and "Jewel Essence® of Synchronicity" aromatherapy blends to attract the right suitor that would want and could afford the business. Within a short period of time, a company approached him with a sound offer to buy the business.

* * *

Olivera was a piano teacher who wanted to increase the number of students for her home-based business. She asked me to do a home consultation and was interested in using "Jewel Essence® of Prosperity." Within that same week, Olivera signed up six new students!

* * *

George worked for a corporate office and felt he did not receive proper recognition for all of his hard work. He used "Jewel Essence® of Synchronicity" and "Jewel Essence® of Recognition," to increase appreciation for his contributions and acknowledgement by his superiors. That same day at work, George was approached by an associate who told him that his name had come up frequently at a recent manager's meeting. George later ran into a Human Resources employee who told George that she had recommended him to a director as an excellent candidate for his department. It suddenly struck George that he was quickly getting the recognition at work that he desired.

* * *

Richard and Sandra have been married for 10 years. Sandra felt that their relationship was becoming stagnant and wanted to add some excitement, including romance. I provided her with Feng Shui tips to enhance the Relationship, Love & Marriage gua of their home, including the use of "Jewel Essence® of Romance" aromatherapy in that area. Since doing so, Sandra says Richard pays more attention to her and she feels more loved again. She is also enjoying more romance in her life, especially in the bedroom!

* * *

Rocio, a single mother of 34, was an Avon representative struggling to make ends meet. She hosted a Feng Shui party in which she learned about and applied the basic foundations and principles of Feng Shui. In addition, she used "Jewel Essence® of Success" and "Jewel Essence® of Synchronicity" aromatherapy to enhance her career. Rocio was delighted to notice an increase in sales shortly thereafter. Then, out of the blue, she was asked to give a motivational talk at an out-of-town convention, all expenses paid.

* * *

Hailey was an 11-year-old girl who wanted to earn extra money. She did not have a "regular" job or a weekly allowance. So Hailey used "Jewel Essence® of Creative Joy" aromatherapy spray to discover creative ways to earn money. After an unexpected party at her home, Hailey decided to collect the recyclable bottles and cans. She took them to the recycling center and received a $30 refund. Not only did Hailey make money, she also helped the environment Since then, she also landed several babysitting jobs, some of which paid double her usual fee!

* * *

Marie had challenging and disharmonious relationships with members of her large family. Her two sisters had been feuding for more than seven years, cutting off communication with each other and causing distress for the entire family. Marie began using "Jewel Essence® of Heart & Soul," a blend of essential oils for the Family & Health gua. Since then, lines of communication between all of her family members opened up again, just in time for the holidays. Marie's two sisters began speaking to each other again. Her younger brother helped put up Christmas lights for their parents, something he does not normally do. And when Marie visited her brother, he shared personal stories about what was currently going on in his life, which he had not done in years. Marie admits that there are a still a few snags in the family dynamics, however she is pleased with the significant progress in the little things that foster positive relationships and a sense of family unity.

* * *

When Carol landed a job as a designer at a kitchen and bath remodeling showroom, her co-workers lamented that they each waited six months before securing clients. Carol decided to be proactive and began using "Jewel Essence® of Synchronicity" aromatherapy to help align the right people at the right time to help her achieve professional success. On the first day of use, Carol picked up a client—the only customer who walked in the showroom that day. This happened day after day as she used the aromatherapy, until Carol had more work than she could handle.

* * *

Julie Ann and her assistant sprayed some of the "Jewel Essence® of Success" before they went to present to one of the management companies that they worked with. To make a long story short, the company bought everything that was presented!

* * *

Stephanie had gone about two months without a single audition. The day after she started using the "Jewel Essence® of Synchronicity" and "Success", her agent called her with a national commercial audition. From that point on, the auditions have been rolling in, including one for NIKE. She is now averaging about two or three a week! She was also contacted by a talent manger, who is interested in representing her and was cast in a short film!

My Own Success Story

Writing my first book was a new and challenging experience for me. So many great ideas were going through my mind (often in my sleep!) as the book began to take shape. Trying to organize my thoughts and focus on actually writing, in addition to maintaining my consulting business and spending time with my family, was a challenge.

So I decided to apply my own methods to writing the book. First, I assessed my situation and identified the areas where I needed strength and improvement: focus, creativity and balance. I created blends of essential oils that would stimulate these areas. Once I applied the aromatherapy blends, I discovered it was much easier to concentrate on writing the book. I could sit down and write for hours at a time with ease. The ideas just flowed! No writer's block. If I forgot to use the aromatherapy blends, I noticed a marked decrease in my concentration and focus. Using *"Jewel Essence® of Health & Harmony"* assisted in maintaining balance in my career and family life as well.

I also wore appropriate crystals to enhance my focus, concentration and creativity. I even placed a large quartz crystal on my desk next to my computer for further enhancement as I did my research and writing.

Shortly after using the *"Jewel Essence® of Success"* aromatherapy blend, I began to see increased success in my business. Once word was out about my line of *"Jewel Essence®"* Feng Shui Aromatherapy, more requests kept coming in. The demand was amazing, and people were experiencing tangible, positive results! As for the success of this book, when clients and fellow colleagues heard I was writing it, they wanted to order copies before it was even published.

The positive outcomes that people, including myself, achieved from using all or part of the Make It Happen Process™ gives me the confidence that the material, techniques and methods of this program are valid. I wish you the same success for your well-being and life goals as well.

For Further Information

The following section includes additional valuable references on Feng Shui and Holistic information. In addition to the glossary and complete appendices on the benefits of Essential Oils and Crystals, you will find two worksheets that will be helpful in implementing Make It Happen Process™ for greater success. I also encourage you to explore the websites, books, and other resources listed in this section.

Glossary

Aromatherapy: The use of the "aroma" of the essential oil for therapy. "Aroma" refers to the unique scent or smell and "therapy" refers to the use of essential oils for healing.

Auspicious: Positive, good.

Bagua Mirror: Special eight sided Feng Shui mirror that is intended to neutralize harmful energies.

Chakra (shakra): A Sanskrit word that means "wheel of light." There are seven main chakras that are associated with the different meridians, starting at the base of the spine and ending at the top of the head.

Chi (chee): A Chinese word for universal life force or cosmic energy. Also known as qi or Prana.

Energy: Another word for Chi (see above).

Feng Shui (feng shway): The art and placement of furniture, doors, windows, etc. to enhance the energy flow throughout the home.

Gua: Area of the home, such as Career, Family & Health, Wealth & Prosperity.

Holistic Health: An alternative health care system to drugs that uses natural methods such as herbs, supplements, massage and emotional clearing. Focus is on the cause of the health issue instead of just the symptoms. Approaches healing on all levels, including physical, mental, emotional and spiritual.

Ketheric: The level of consciousness of pure energy and spirit.

Meridian: Pathways of energy that are interactive with the chakras. These pathways are also where Acupuncturists place needles to balance the body's energy.

Secret Arrows: Negative energies that come from sharp pointing objects or corners, such as corners from a roof or from walls and furniture.

Synchronicity: Being in the right place at the right time can assist all aspects of our life to flow easily and bring about good fortune.

Tai Chi (tie chee): As it relates to Feng Shui, it is the center of the bagua and associated with Health & Unity. It is represented by the Yin/Yang symbol, which represents harmony, balance and overall well-being.

Vortex: A whirlpool of energy.

Yang: Associated with male and strong energy.

Yin: Associated with female and softer energy.

Appendix 1:
Benefits of Essential Oils

Bergamot: Facilitates strength, power, confidence and motivation. Relieves feelings of anxiety, stress and tension.

Cedarwood: Promotes self-control, self-image, confidence and power. *Caution: Avoid during pregnancy.*

Chamomile: Facilitates peace, joy and relaxation.

Roman: Balances the emotions.

Cinnamon Bark: Believed to have a frequency that attracts wealth. *Caution: Avoid during pregnancy.*

Clove: Promotes courage and protection. *Caution: Avoid during pregnancy.*

Cypress: Produces a feeling of grounding and security. Facilitates confidence, strength and courage.

Eucalyptus globulus: Facilitates concentration, logical thought and positive change. Supports and encourages purification, health and well-being.

Frankincense: Promotes meditation and spiritual awareness. Facilitates wisdom, inspiration, performance and emotional stability. Promotes a positive attitude. *Caution: Avoid during pregnancy.*

Geranium: Facilitates creativity, security and balance. Promotes feelings of well-being and peace. Uplifting and assists in stabilizing the emotions.

Ginger: Helps to provide direction and purpose by facilitating courage, confidence and strength. May influence money.

Jasmine: Assists in elevating the emotions. May enhance wisdom and intuition. Acts as an aphrodisiac.

Juniper: Induces feelings of peace, love and health. May promote one's spiritual awareness. *Caution: Avoid during pregnancy.*

Lavender: Promotes relaxation, calmness and emotional/physical balancing. Encourages health, inner peace, compassion and love. Promotes a sense of well-being. Facilitates acceptance and assistance.

Lemon: Enhances focus, clarity and concentration. Uplifting, combats depression. Enhances purification. Stimulates physical energy. Promotes healing and health. Encourages communication and acceptance of help.

Lemongrass: Aids in purification. Enhances psychic awareness.

Mandarin: Uplifts, revitalizes and refreshes. Facilitates happiness.

Myrrh: Uplifting. Facilitates spiritual awareness. *Caution: Avoid during pregnancy.*

Neroli: Promotes confidence and courage. Facilitates peace and joy. Enhances sensuality.

Orange: Uplifting, enhancing feelings of joy, contentment, happiness and light heartedness.

Oregano: Produces a sense of security. *Caution: Avoid during pregnancy.*

Patchouli: Promotes relaxation, alleviates feelings of anxiety.

Peppermint: Stimulating, and promotes concentration. Helps to reduce mental fatigue and apathy. Promotes acceptance and communication. *Caution: Avoid during pregnancy.*

Petitgrain: Uplifting. Enhances memory. Eases mental fatigue and helps to clear confusion.

Pine: Facilitates forgiveness for self and others, acceptance of help, love and understanding. Reduces anxiety and rejuvenates the whole body.

Rose: Stimulating and uplifting, producing a feeling of well-being. Enhances feelings of harmony, forgiveness, love and compassion. Acts like an aphrodisiac.

Rosemary: Enhances memory. Believed to attract wealth. *Caution: Avoid during pregnancy.*

Rosewood: Produces a sense of relaxation and peace.

Sage: Stimulating, and promotes concentration. Helps to reduce mental fatigue and apathy. Promotes acceptance and communication. *Caution: Avoid during pregnancy.*

Sandalwood: Facilitates self-awareness, balance, and connection. Facilitates joy, self-esteem and self-image. Facilitates balance, unity and healing. Helps to neutralize manipulation, obsession and aggression. Assists in calming and balancing the emotions.

Spruce: Grounding, producing the feeling of balance. Facilitates the release of emotional blocks. Believed to attract wealth.

Tangerine: Promotes a sense of calmness, reducing anxiety.

Vetiver: Reduces stress by being emotionally calming, stabilizing and grounding.

Ylang ylang: Facilitates sensuality and sexuality. Assists in relationships. Acts as an aphrodisiac. Promotes feelings of peace, joy, self-love, and confidence. Promotes unification. Reduces resentment, jealousy and frustration.

Information provided in this book has been applied to Feng Shui and the different areas of your life by the author from the following resources:

Essential Oils Desk Reference, 3rd Ed., compiled and published by Essential Science Publishing, Provo, Utah 2004.

Higley, Connie and Alan, *Reference Guide for Essential Oils*. Abundant Health, KS, 1998.

Appendix 2: Benefits of Crystals

AMBER:
Usually yellow-brown to golden fossilized resin (petrified tree sap), can also be green, red or blue

Chakras: Root, Sacral and Solar Plexus

Energetic Influence: Absorbs and transmutes negative energy to positive.

- *Career:* Provides grounding and protection.

AMAZONITE:
Usually light turquoise, also can be yellow, white or gray

Chakras: Heart and Throat

Energetic Influence: Emits a soothing energy, especially for emotional processes and worries.

- *Creativity & Children:* Assists in communications related to love.

AMETHYST:
From transparent pale lavender to deep purple quartz

Chakra: Activates Crown Chakra

Energetic Influence:

- *Career:* Enhances strength & stability.
- *Knowledge & Self-Cultivation:* As a stone for meditation, it enhances relaxation, meditation and spiritual insight.
- *Wealth & Prosperity:* May help business affairs prosper. By focusing love and gratitude into the amethyst, you may attract abundance or prosperity in other aspects of your life as well.

AQUAMARINE:
Transparent pale blue

Chakra: Activates and cleanses the Throat Chakra.

Energetic Influence: Known as a "stone of courage."

- *Knowledge & Self-Cultivation:* Facilitates calmness, peace and meditation. Assists in attuning one to higher spiritual awareness.

- *Helpful People & Travel:* Facilitates higher levels of communication.

AVENTURINE:
Usually a green quartz, although it can be other colors

Chakra: Activates and clears the Heart Chakra.

Energetic Influence:

- *Family & Health:* Aids in emotional stability.

- *Creativity & Children:* Enhances creativity and motivation in activities.

- *Helpful People & Travel:* A stone of opportunity and good luck.

- *Tai Chi: Health & Unity:* Assists in balancing the male/female energies.

AZURITE:
Indigo, can range from opaque light to dark blue

Chakra: Third Eye Chakra provides guidance in the pursuit of the heavenly self.

Energetic Influence: is a stone of heaven.

- *Career:* Aids in finding direction.

- *Knowledge & Self-Cultivation:* Assists in meditation. Calms the mind to assist in reaching the state of "no mind."

- *Creativity & Children:* Enhances creativity and compassion.

BLACK OBSIDIAN:
Black volcanic glass

Chakra: Root

Energetic Influence: Acts as a shield and transmutes negative energies to positive energy.

- *Career:* Promotes grounding and emotional security. Protects emotional draining from others, sharpens visions and helps with transitions.

- *Creativity & Children:* Induces creativity in all activities.

BLACK ONYX:

Black

Chakra: Root

Energetic Influence:

- *Career:* Assists in making wise decisions. Encourages good fortune and happiness.

BLOODSTONE:

Green with red flecks

Chakras: Root, Heart

Energetic Influence:

- *Career:* Known as a "stone of courage," it enhances abilities and talents and aids in the process of making decisions.

- *Creativity & Children:* Enhances creativity.

BLUE LACE AGATE:

Blue with white lace pattern or bands and stripes

Chakras: Activates the Heart, Throat, Third Eye and Crown Chakras.

Energetic Influence:

- *Knowledge & Self-Cultivation:* Assists in reaching higher states of awareness and spiritual realms.

CARNELIAN:

Translucent orange, red, red-brown

Chakras: Good for the Base, Sacral, Solar and Heart Chakras.

Energetic Influence:

- *Career:* Has a grounding effect. Helps to stimulate courage, physical energy and physical power.

- *Fame & Reputation:* Stimulates inspiration.

- *Creativity & Children:* Enhances creativity and compassion.

- *Tai Chi: Health & Unity:* Helps to stabilize the energy in the home.

CELESTITE:

Usually translucent blue, can also be white, yellow, orange, red and red-brown

Chakras: Throat

Energetic Influence:

- *Knowledge & Self-Cultivation:* Assists in mental activities.
- *Helpful People & Travel:* Aids in ease of communication.
- *Tai Chi: Health & Unity:* Balances the yin and yang energies. Attracts harmony and calmness.

CINNABAR:

Usually red, can also be red-brown, gray

Chakra: Root

Energetic Influence: Stimulates power, dignity and vitality.

- *Wealth & Prosperity:* As a "merchant's stone," it assists in accumulating and maintaining wealth.

CITRINE:

Translucent yellow, yellow-orange, golden brown quartz

Chakras: Helps to activate and energize the Sacral and Solar Plexus chakras. Also stimulates the Crown Chakra.

Energetic Influence: Clears negative energy, never needs clearing itself.

- *Career:* Provides a sense of stability and emotional balance. Facilitates a rational approach toward challenges.
- *Family & Health:* Helps to smooth over group and family problems, thus produces cohesiveness within that group.
- *Creativity & Children:* Stimulates intuition and creativity.
- *Wealth & Prosperity:* As a "merchant's stone," it is thought to assist in accumulating and maintaining a state of wealth.
- *Tai Chi: Health & Unity:* Provides a sense of stability and emotional balance.

DIAMOND:

Usually colorless

Chakra: Crown

Energetic Influence: Use with other gemstones to further enhance their qualities.

- *Wealth & Prosperity:* Enhances manifestation of abundance in all areas of life.
- *Creativity & Children:* Inspires imagination, inventiveness and creativity.

EMERALD:

Deep green

Chakra: Heart

Energetic Influence:

- *Knowledge & Self-Cultivation:* Enhances memory and intelligence and wisdom.
- *Creativity & Children:* Enhances creativity and speech.
- *Tai Chi: Health & Unity:* Brings harmony to all aspects of one's life.

ELESTIAL CRYSTALS:

Translucent clear

Chakras: All

Energetic Influence: Known as a "stone of enchantment."

- *Fame & Reputation:* Enhances the power of personal expression and potential.
- *Helpful People & Travel:* Assists bringing the heart and the intellect into synchronicity and in alignment with the spiritual realm.

FLOURITE:

Can be any color, however the most common colors are green and purple

Chakras: All, especially Heart, Third Eye and Crown Chakras.

Energetic Influence: Known as a "stone of discernment," it discourages chaos and disruption.

- *Knowledge & Self-Cultivation:* Enhances understanding, mental concentration and capacity.
- *Tai Chi: Health & Unity:* Enhances the perfect ideal of health and emotional well-being.

GARNET:

Usually a deep rosy-red, can also be pink or purple

Chakras: Stimulates Root (base) and Crown Chakras.

Energetic Influence: Transmutes negative energy into positive energy.

- *Career:* Known as a "stone of commitment" to oneself, others and purpose.

- *Family & Health / Tai Chi: Health & Unity:* Known as a "stone of health."

- *Creativity & Children:* Assists creative powers into manifestation.

GOLD:

Usually golden yellow, orange-red or silver-white

Chakras: Cleanses and balances the Heart Chakra. Opens and activates the Third Eye and Crown Chakras.

Energetic Influence: Attracts happiness.

- *Family & Health, Relationships, Love & Marriage:* Attracts cooperation and receptivity.

- *Wealth & Prosperity:* Attracts wealth.

- *Fame & Reputation:* Attracts honors.

- *Creativity & Children:* Attracts cooperation and receptivity.

HEMATITE:

Although usually steel gray to black, it can also be brown-red and red

Chakra: Root (base)

Energetic Influence: Acts as a shield and dissolves negative energy. Known as the "stone for the mind."

- *Career:* Provides a state of mind that allows grounding, harmony and emotional clarity.

- *Knowledge & Self-Cultivation:* Provides a calming atmosphere, while at the same time enhancing memory and mental attunement. Helps to sort out things in the mind.

- *Fame & Reputation:* Encourages one to reach for the stars.

- *Tai Chi: Health & Unity:* Helps balance yin/yang energies, the body, mind and spirit.

JADE:

Usually green, also can be just about any other color

Chakras: All, each corresponding to the color of the chakra.

Energetic Influence: Transmutes negative energy into positive energy. Facilitates release of suppressed emotions through the dream process.

- *Career:* Known as a "dream stone," it helps one to realize their devotion to their purpose. Assists in confidence, self-sufficiency, self-reliance and self-assuredness.

- *Knowledge & Self-Cultivation:* Enhances courage, clarity and tranquility of the mind.

- *Family & Health (green jade):* Promotes understanding and cohesiveness of groups. Helps to provide the ability to bring together and improve dysfunctional relationships.

- *Fame & Reputation:* Assists in the transformation of one's dreams into physical reality. Inspires ambition toward completion of objectives. Helps to release one's limitation and to actualize aspirations to achieve limitless achievements.

- *Tai Chi: Health & Unity:* Known as a "stone of harmony," it facilitates peace between the emotional, mental and physical.

LAPIS LAZULI:

Blue to deep blue

Chakras: Throat and Third Eye

Energetic Influence: Known as a "stone of total awareness," it assists expansion of intellectual capacity and awareness.

- *Knowledge & Self-Cultivation:* Enhances mental endurance, wisdom to understand information, insight and good judgment.

- *Family & Health / Relationships, Love & Marriage:* Helps relationships to be successful.

MALACHITE:

Green, dark green with light green bands

Chakras: Stimulates Throat and Heart Chakras. Clears and activates all chakras.

Energetic Influence: Known as a "stone of transformation," it helps one in transformational changes and purification.

- *Career / Fame & Reputation:* Assists in achieving desired goal.

- *Wealth & Prosperity:* Enhances good fortune and success in business.

- *Creativity & Children:* Protects your creative ideas.

- *Relationships, Love & Marriage:* Represents loyalty in love, friendship and partnerships.

PINK TOURMALINE:

Transparent spike-like pink

Chakras: Stimulates the Heart and Crown, connecting love and spirituality.

Energetic Influence:

- *Family & Health / Relationships, Love & Marriage:* Receiving and giving love joyfully.

- *Creativity & Children:* Promotes creativity. Encourages feelings of peace and joy during times of change and growth. Assists in the ability to receive and give love joyfully.

QUARTZ, CLEAR:

Clear

Chakras: Balances and stabilizes all chakras.

Energetic Influence: Known as a "stone of power," it enhances creation of power.

- *Knowledge & Self-Cultivation:* Enhances mental clarity, meditation and spiritual development.

- *Helpful People & Travel:* Facilitates communication with the helpful people in your life, such as spiritual masters, teachers and healers.

- *Tai Chi: Health & Unity:* Has a natural tendency for harmony.

RED CORAL:

Opaque red

Chakra: Root (base)

Energetic Influence:

- *Career / Fame & Reputation:* Stimulates the energetic pursuits of goals.

RED JASPER:

Opaque red-orange

Chakra: Root (base)

Energetic Influence:

- *Career:* Promotes grounding and helps to reduce fears and insecurities.

RHODOCROSITE:

Translucent pink with lacy designs

Chakras: Root, Sacral and Heart

Energetic Influence:

- *Relationships, Love & Marriage / Family & Health:* Known as a "stone of love and balance," it enhances love for self and others. Eases emotional pain.

RHODONITE:

Usually pink to rose-red, can also be brown-red, black, yellow and green

Chakra: Root, Sacral and Heart

Energetic Influence: Enhances self-worth, self-confidence and self-esteem.

- *Family & Health / Relationships, Love & Marriage:* Known as a "stone of love," it resonates to unconditional love.

ROSE QUARTZ:

Translucent and opaque pink

Chakras: Heart and Crown

Energetic Influence: Facilitates feelings of relaxation, calmness, tranquility and inner peace.

- *Family & Health / Relationships, Love & Marriage:* As a "stone of gentle love," it enhances feelings and abilities to give and receive love and compassion, including self-love.
- *Tai Chi: Health & Unity:* Balances the yin and yang energies.

RUBY:

Medium to dark pink, crimson red, red-orange

Chakras: Root and Heart

Energetic Influence: Courage

- *Wealth & Prosperity:* Promotes stability of wealth.
- *Relationships, Love & Marriage:* Increases feelings of love and compassion.

SAPPHIRE:

Usually light blue to deep indigo

Chakras: Throat and Third Eye

Energetic Influence:

- *Helpful People & Travel:* Assists in communication.

SMOKY QUARTZ:

Light to dark smoky gray or brown quartz

Chakra: Root and Solar Plexus

Energetic Influence: Assists in transforming and dissolving negative emotional patterns and blockages.

- *Career:* Good for grounding. Known as a "stone of cooperation," it enhances unification of thoughts directed toward the same goal.
- *Knowledge & Self-Cultivation:* Enhances mental clarity and meditation.
- *Fame & Reputation:* Helps you to achieve your highest aspirations and hopes.
- *Creativity & Children:* Enhances joy of living, helps to regulate creativity in business.
- *Tai Chi: Health & Unity:* Facilitates balancing of the yin-yang energies.

SODALITE:

Usually dark blue with white lines

Chakras: Third Eye, Throat

Energetic Influence: Assists in eliminating confusion, replacing your inner doubts, fears and anxieties with white light and transformation.

- *Career:* Helps provide direction of purpose with light heartedness.
- *Creativity & Children:* Can enhance truthfulness in emotions, allowing one to recognize and verbalize true feelings.
- *Knowledge & Self-Cultivation:* Assists in rational mental processes.

TIGER EYE:

Usually golden brown with golden highlights

Chakras: Best at Solar Plexus, Third Eye and Base Chakras.

Energetic Influence:

- *Career:* Facilitates self-confidence, inner strength and stability to be more grounded.
- *Wealth & Prosperity:* Attracts and maintains wealth.
- *Creativity & Children:* Enhances creativity and practical decision-making.
- *Tai Chi: Health & Unity:* Balances the yin and yang energies.

TOURMALINE:

Transparent spike-like black, green, pink

Chakras: All

Energetic Influence:

- *Any Color—Fame & Reputation:* Attracts inspiration and self-confidence.

- *Any Color—Tai Chi: Health & Unity:* Balances the yin and yang energies.

- *Black—Career:* Acts as a protective shield against negativity from self and others.

- *Green—Wealth & Prosperity:* Attracts abundance & prosperity.

- *Pink—Relationships, Love & Marriage:* Joyfully receiving and giving out love, assists in releasing destructive tendencies, thus allowing for feelings of love and joy for life.

TURQUOISE:

Opaque greenish blue

Chakras: Throat and Third Eye

Energetic Influence: Enhances physical balance and confidence.

- *Knowledge & Self-Cultivation:* Facilitates mental relaxation, stress reduction and attunement.

- *Wealth & Prosperity:* Attracts prosperity and abundance.

Information provided in this book has been applied to Feng Shui and the different areas of your life by the author from the following resource:

Melody, *Love is in the Earth: A Kaleidoscope of Crystals*. Earth-Love Publishing House, Wheatridge, CO, 1995.

MAKE IT HAPPEN PROCESS™ WORKSHEET

Gua/Life Issue: _____

Date Started: _____

What is your current situation?

_____
_____
_____

What would you like to enhance or improve in this area?

_____
_____
_____

What did you do?

☐ TLC PROCESS™

Positive Affirmation(s):

_____
_____
_____

☐ AROMATHERAPY FOR BODY   ☐ AROMATHERAPY FOR HOME

Name of blend/essential oils: _____

☐ CRYSTAL (Name/Type/Color)_____

Your written affirmation in this area/gua of the home: _____

What were the results?

_____
_____
_____

Reflections:

_____
_____
_____

PROGRESS CHART

Gua/Life Issue: _____

Date Started: _____

Mark a ✔ each time you do an affirmation or aromatherapy application.

DATE	AFFIRMATION	AROMATHERAPY		DATE	AFFIRMATION	AROMATHERAPY	
		GUA	BODY			GUA	BODY

Bibliography & Recommended Reading

Bowman, Catherine, *Crystal Awareness*. Llewellyn Publications, St. Paul, MN, 1987.

Brennan, Barbara, *Hands of Light, A Guide to Healing Through the Human Energy Field*. Bantam Books, NY, 1987.

Bruyere, Rosalyn, *Wheels of Light, Chakras, Auras, and The Healing Energy of the Body*. Fireside, New York, 1994.

Carlo, George, Dr., *Cell Phones, Invisible Hazards of the Wireless Age*. Carroll & Graf Publishers, New York, NY, 2001.

Collins, Terah Kathryn, *Home Design with Feng Shui A-Z*. Hay House Publishing, Carlsbad, CA, 1999.

Collins, Terah Kathryn, *The Western Guide to Feng Shui*. Hay House Publishing, Carlsbad, CA, 1996.

Collins, Terah Kathryn, *The Western Guide to Feng Shui; Creating Balance, Harmony, and Prosperity in Your Environment*. Hay House Publishing, Carlsbad, CA, 1996.

Collins, Terah Kathryn, *The Western Guide to Feng Shui for Prosperity*. Hay House Publishing, Carlsbad, CA, 2002.

Collins, Terah Kathryn, *The Western Guide to Feng Shui for Romance*. Hay House Publishing, Carlsbad, CA, 2004.

Collins, Terah Kathryn, *The Western Guide to Feng Shui; Room by Room*. Hay House Publishing, Carlsbad, CA. 1999.

Cooksley, Valerie, *Aromatherapy, A Lifetime Guide to Healing with Essential Oils*. Prentice Hall, NJ, 1996.

Diamond, John, M.D., *Life Energy, Using the Meridians to Unlock the Hidden Power of Your Emotions*. Paragon House, St. Paul, MN, 1985.

Durlacher, James, D.C., *Freedom From Fear Forever*. Van Ness Publishing Company, AZ, 1995.

Essential Oils Desk Reference, 3rd Ed., compiled and published by Essential Science Publishing, Provo, Utah 2004.

Kingston, Karen, *Clear Your Clutter with Feng Shui*. Broadway Books, New York, NY, 1998.

Kopec, DAK, Ph.D., IDEC, CHES, *Environmental Psychology for Design*. Fairchild Books, New York, NY, 2006.

Grabhorn, Lynn, *Excuse Me, Your Life is Waiting, the Astonishing Power of Feelings*. Hampton Roads Publishing Company, Inc., Charlottesville, VA, 2000.

Gunther, Bernard, *Energy Ecstasy and Your Seven Vital Chakras*. New Castle Publishing, Inc., CA, 1983.

Hay, Louise, *Heal Your Body A-Z, The Mental Causes for Physical Illness and the Way to Overcome Them*. Hay House, Inc., Carlsbad, CA, 1998.

Higley, Connie and Alan, *Reference Guide for Essential Oils*. Abundant Health, KS, 1998.

Judith, Anodea, *Wheels of Life, A User's Guide to the Chakra System*. Llewellyn Publications, St. Paul, MN, 1987.

Lin, Jami, *The Essence of Feng Shui, Balancing Your Body, Home, and Your Life with Fragrance*. Hay House Publishing, Carlsbad, CA, 1998.

Linn, Denise, *Sacred Space, Clearing and Enhancing the Energy of Your Home*. Ballantine Books, New York, 1995.

Maggiore, Evana, *Fashion Feng Shui, The Power of Dressing with Intention*. Mansion Publishing LTD, 2007.

Mein, Carolyn L., D.C., *Releasing Emotional Patterns with Essential Oils*. VisionWare Press, CA, 2002.

Melody, *Love is in the Earth: A Kaleidoscope of Crystals*. Earth-Love Publishing House, Wheatridge, CO, 1995.

McLaren, Karla, *Your Aura & Your Chakras, The Owner's Manual*. Weiser Books, Maine, 1998.

Myss, Caroline, Ph.D., *Anatomy of the Spirit, The Seven Stages of Power and Healing*. Crown Publishers, Inc., New York, 1996.

Pinsky, Mark, *The EMF Book, What You Should Know About Electromagnetic Fields, Electromagnetic radiation, and Your Health*. Warner Books, Inc. New York, 1995.

Poe, "Rahasya" Wm and Lemos, Dhara, *The 12 Spiritual Laws of Recovery and Meditations for the 12-Step Program*. Ist Books Library, Bloomington, IN 2003.

Raphael, Katrina, *Crystal Enlightenment, The Transforming Properties of Crystals and Healing Stones*. Aurora Press, Santa Fe, NM, 1985.

Raphael, Katrina, *Crystal Healing, The Therapeutic Application of Crystals and Stones*. Aurora Press, Santa Fe, NM, 1987.

Sullivan, Kevin, *The Crystal Handbook*. Nal Penguin Inc., New York, New York, 1987.

Tan, Richard, L.Ac., and Warnke, Cheryl, L.Ac., *Shower of Jewels, Feng Shui: An Amusing Yet Practical Guide to Ancient Principles of Placement and Geoenergy Manipulation*. San Diego, 1996.

Thie, John, D.C. and Mathew, M.Ed., *Touch for Health, A Practical Guide to Natural Health with Acupressure Touch*. DeVorss Publications, CA, 2005.

Troyer, Patricia, *Crystal Personalities, A Quick Reference to Special Forms of Quartz*. Stone People Publishing Company, 1995.

Truman, Karol, *Feelings Buried Alive Never Die...* Olympus Distributing, Las Vegas, Nevada, 1991.

Whitaker, Charlene, *Gems of Wisdom*. Cosmic Connection, 1987.

White, Ruth, *Using Your Chakras, A New Approach to Healing Your Life*. Samuel Weiser, Inc., York Beach, ME, 2000.

Worwood, Susan, *Essential Aromatherapy. A Pocket Guide to Essential Oils and Aromatherapy*. New World Library, CA, 1995.

Ziegler, Holly, *Sell Your Home FASTER with Feng Shui*. Dragon Chi™ Publications, Arroyo Grande, CA, 2001.

Ziegler, Holly, *Buy Your Home SMARTER with Feng Shui*. Dragon Chi™ Publications, Arroyo Grande, CA, 2004.

About the Author

JEN LEONG, MA, HHP, NC, Author, Feng Shui Consultant, Holistic Health Professional (HHP), Speaker & Educator, and proprietor of Wellness by Design, brings more than 22 years of combined experience, training, and expertise to her wellness and Feng Shui practice. She has a unique ability to integrate Feng Shui and Holistic Health, allowing her to empower clients with the techniques and tools necessary to bring health and harmony into all aspects of life.

Jen Leong is the author of *Make It Happen with Feng Shui: Attract What YOU Want!* and the *Make It Happen with Feng Shui* Series. These are more than your ordinary books. These are personal resource guides with groundbreaking information and easy, practical methods to enhance your well-being and attract what you want in life. She has uniquely integrated the ancient wisdom of Feng Shui, aromatherapy, crystals and emotional clearing in these all-in-one, easy-to-use reference guides. They include exclusive charts, graphics and worksheets. Discover how you can apply these tools to enhance your life, well-being and attract what you want in life.

Jen facilitates environmental healing by bringing balance and harmony into your home or office through the art of Feng Shui. She has training in Classical, Compass and Form School. A graduate of the Western School of Feng Shui, Jen has personally trained under Terah Kathryn Collins. She has also studied with Master Peter Leung with the School of Chinese Metaphysics and Yasha Jampolsky with the Green Planet School of Feng Shui. Jen furthered her Feng Shui training and studied Space Clearing with Denise Linn, Feng Shui Real Estate with Holly Ziegler and Fashion Feng Shui with Evana Maggiore. She is also a Red Ribbon Professional Member of the International Feng Shui Guild.

Jen is also a nutritional consultant (NC), specializing in Nutritional Therapy. She has extensive training in the use of therapeutic herbs and high quality supplements from industry-leading organizations including Apex, Metagenics, Premiere Research Lab, Designs for Health, and the International Foundation for Nutrition and Health. She also has extensive training in Kinesiology (muscle testing) to find and remove the cause of self-sabotage and symptoms of dis-ease.

Jen gives presentations and teaches workshops on Feng Shui, including unique information from her book. She has also been featured on TV to discuss Feng Shui, her books and services.

Jen received her degrees in Wildlife Biology from U.C. Davis, Teaching Credential, San Diego State University, Masters in Exercise Physiology, San Diego State University, and Holistic Health training from Healing Hands School of Holistic Health and other holistic institutions. Jen continues her training in Feng Shui and Holistic Health on a continuous basis.

Resources

For information on these products, services and helpful people, go to **www.JenLeong.com** or call **858 618-3833**.

PRODUCTS

- *Jewel Essence®* Feng Shui Aromatherapy
- Aromatherapy
- Crystals
- EMF Protection Products
- Feng Shui Products

SERVICES

- Feng Shui
- Consultations (Business and Residential)
- Speaking Engagements
- Workshops
- "Harmony at Home" Parties
- "Fashion Feng Shui" Parties
  Dress for Succes
- Space Clearing
- Make It Happen Process™
  Clearing the Way
  Setting Your Intentions to Attract What You Want
- Emotional Clearing—TLC Process™

HELPFUL PEOPLE

For a list of Helpful People in the San Diego area, please visit **www.JenLeong.com.**

INTRODUCING...

Jewel Essence®
Feng Shui Aromatherapy

Uniquely Formulated to Enhance the 9 Areas of Your Home & Body.

Wellness by Design is pleased to introduce *Jewel Essence®*, a unique line of Feng Shui Aromatherapy specially formulated with blends of *100% pure essential oils* and infused with the appropriate healing chakra sounds and crystals to enhance each of the nine areas in your life:

Success	*Prosperity*	*Romance*
Recognition	*Synchronicity*	*Creative Joy*
Health & Harmony	*Heart & Soul*	*Wisdom*
	Space Clearing	

Each bottle contains gemstones to enhance your results. These all-natural blends are available in two forms for each area or gua of the home and body:

Visit our website for pricing!

AROMAMIST®
An aromatic room spray to enhance each gua of the home.

AROMACHAKRAOIL®
A unique blend formulated for the chakras of your body to enhance your life and well-being.

ORDER TODAY!
Visit our website for more kits
wwwJenLeong.com
858.618.3833

WELLNESS by **DESIGN**

JEN LEONG MA, HHP, NC
Feng Shui & Holistic Health Consultant, Author

Visit **www.JenLeong.com** for current prices.

Count the Ways to Better Well-Being

Wellness by Design brings you many exciting tools to enhance the Feng Shui experience for yourself or your clientele. Call or go online to place your order today.

Book

Make It Happen with Feng Shui

Author Jen Leong reveals easy, practical methods to attract what you want with this all-in-one, easy-to-use reference guide.

Book & AromaMist® Starter Kit

Start enhancing your life and well-being now with this specially priced Feng Shui Wellness Starter Kit, including *Make It Happen With Feng Shui* book and your choice of one *Jewel Essence®* AromaMist® aromatherapy blend.

Feng Shui Jewel Essence® Kits

SUCCESS KIT
- Prosperity
- Success
- Synchronicity

RECOGNITION KIT
- Recognition
- Success
- Synchronicity

ROMANCE KIT
- Romance
- Creative Joy
- Synchronicity

FAMILY KIT
- Heart & Soul
- Creative Joy
- Health & Harmony

Buy More & SAVE!

WELLNESS by DESIGN

JEN LEONG MA, HHP, NC
Feng Shui & Holistic Health Consultant, Author

ORDER TODAY!
Visit our website for more kits

www.JenLeong.com
858.618.3833

Notes

Notes

CPSIA information can be obtained
at www.ICGtesting.com
Printed in the USA
LVHW101328250221
679941LV00014B/257

9 780979 625633